Cambridge Elements

Elements in Global Philosophy of Religion
edited by
Yujin Nagasawa
University of Oklahoma

THE NOTION OF VITALITY IN AFRICAN PHILOSOPHY OF RELIGION

Aribiah David Attoe
University of the Witwatersrand and The Conversational School of Philosophy, Nigeria

Amara Esther Chimakonam
University of Fort Hare and The Conversational School of Philosophy, Nigeria

Shaftesbury Road, Cambridge CB2 8EA, United Kingdom

One Liberty Plaza, 20th Floor, New York, NY 10006, USA

477 Williamstown Road, Port Melbourne, VIC 3207, Australia

314–321, 3rd Floor, Plot 3, Splendor Forum, Jasola District Centre, New Delhi – 110025, India

103 Penang Road, #05–06/07, Visioncrest Commercial, Singapore 238467

Cambridge University Press is part of Cambridge University Press & Assessment, a department of the University of Cambridge.

We share the University's mission to contribute to society through the pursuit of education, learning and research at the highest international levels of excellence.

www.cambridge.org
Information on this title: www.cambridge.org/9781009505994

DOI: 10.1017/9781009506021

© Aribiah David Attoe and Amara Esther Chimakonam 2025

This work is in copyright. It is subject to statutory exceptions and to the provisions of relevant licensing agreements; with the exception of the Creative Commons version the link for which is provided below, no reproduction of any part of this work may take place without the written permission of Cambridge University Press.

An online version of this work is published at doi.org/10.1017/9781009506021 under a Creative Commons Open Access licence CC-BY-NC 4.0 which permits re-use, distribution and reproduction in any medium for non-commercial purposes providing appropriate credit to the original work is given and any changes made are indicated. To view a copy of this licence, visit https://creativecommons.org/licenses/by-nc/4.0

All versions of this work may contain content reproduced under license from third parties. Permission to reproduce this third-party content must be obtained from these third-parties directly.

When citing this work, please include a reference to the DOI 10.1017/9781009506021

First published 2025

A catalogue record for this publication is available from the British Library

ISBN 978-1-009-50599-4 Hardback
ISBN 978-1-009-50600-7 Paperback
ISSN 2976-5749 (online)
ISSN 2976-5730 (print)

Cambridge University Press & Assessment has no responsibility for the persistence or accuracy of URLs for external or third-party internet websites referred to in this publication and does not guarantee that any content on such websites is, or will remain, accurate or appropriate.

For EU product safety concerns, contact us at Calle de José Abascal, 56, 1°, 28003 Madrid, Spain, or email eugpsr@cambridge.org

The Notion of Vitality in African Philosophy of Religion

Elements in Global Philosophy of Religion

DOI: 10.1017/9781009506021
First published online: October 2025

Aribiah David Attoe
University of the Witwatersrand and The Conversational School of Philosophy, Nigeria

Amara Esther Chimakonam
University of Fort Hare and The Conversational School of Philosophy, Nigeria

Author for correspondence: Aribiah David Attoe, aribiahdavidattoe@gmail.com

Abstract: Since the early works of scholars like Alexis Kagame and Placide Tempels, discussions on the concept of vitality in African philosophy have acquired many dimensions. With scholars like Noah Dzobo and Thaddeus Metz projecting it as a grounding for human values and dignity, Aribiah Attoe and Yolanda Mlungwana each exploring vitalist conceptions of meaning in life, and Ada Agada approaching vitality from a proto-panpsychist/consolationist perspective. Indeed, vitality features as an important concept in African philosophy of religion. This Element contributes to the discourse on vitality in African philosophy of religion by providing a critical overview of some traditional interpretations of the concept from the Bantu, Yoruba, and Igbo religious/philosophical worldviews. Furthermore, it explores how the concept of vitality features in discussions of ethics, dignity, and meaning in life. Finally, the Element provides a critique of the concept based on the interventions of Innocent Asouzu, Metz, and Bernard Matolino. This title is also available as open access on Cambridge Core.

Keywords: African Philosophy, vitality, dignity, meaning, liveliness

© Aribiah David Attoe and Amara Esther Chimakonam 2025

ISBNs: 9781009505994 (HB), 9781009506007 (PB), 9781009506021 (OC)
ISSNs: 2976-5749 (online), 2976-5730 (print)

Contents

Introduction   1

Part I   Some Core Ideas About the Nature of Vitality: Metaphysics and Religion   3

1   Vitality and Bantu Ontology   3

2   Vitality and the Concept of *Ase* in Yoruba Ontology   11

3   Vitality and '*Ndu*' in Igbo Ontology   19

Part II   Vitalist Approaches in African Philosophy of Religion   22

4   Vitality and Ethics   22

5   Vitality and Dignity   30

6   Vitality and Meaning in Life   35

Part III   Some Critiques of the Vital Force Theory   44

7   A Racial Foundation   44

8   The Supernaturalist Critique   46

9   Critiquing the Naturalist View   48

Conclusion   52

References   53

Introduction

When we observe individuals and other living things in the world, there is this inescapable assumption that there is something present in every living thing that animates them and causes them to display *life*.[1] For millennia, human beings have described this animating principle in various ways – soul, spirit, vitality/vital force, and so on – and despite the many advances of science (especially in the area of neuroscience), the inescapability of this assumption yet remains, taking hold in the seemingly non-reducible notion of qualia – the subjective, conscious, and unique experience of life that is hard to reduce to the material components of the human body.

When Tempels began his missionary work in the Congo, it was quite clear that the anonymous traditional philosophers and theologians of the Bantu system of thought,[2] whom he obviously had encounters with and whose ideas he purportedly restated in his work, also held this assumption to be true – that there exists this imperceptible force that animated living things. Even further, this force was thought of as permeating other inanimate things, but to a lower degree. As research into vitality began to increase, strong traces of the view started to emerge in other philosophical traditions in Southern and Western Africa (Nalwamba & Buitendag, 2017). And so we see, in the concept of vitality, a traditional religious and philosophical viewpoint that permeates aspects of various cultural traditions (like the Igbo, Yoruba, and Bantu traditions). Thus, despite the controversies associated with the view, vitality remains an important concept in African theology and African philosophy of religion.

What has followed the theoretical development of the notion of vitality is its application in various areas of ethical concern. Some, like Motsamai Molefe (2017), have applied the theory of vitality to questions relating to understanding what constitutes human dignity and as a more plausible/alternative framework to the Divine Command Theory. Others like Mlungwana (2020) and Attoe

---

[1] From the outset, it is important to acknowledge the underrepresentation of women in the theories explored here. This underrepresentation is because the theorisation and interpretation of vitality in African philosophy are strongly constituted and dominated by the perspectives of male African philosophers. We have searched tirelessly to find relevant works that meaningfully engaged the concept of vitality from the perspectives of female African philosophers but have yet to find any. This is not to say that female *African* philosophers are not particularly aware of the notion of vital force in African philosophy. We must also mention, however, that there are some attempts to engage the African notion of vitality by female scholars from Europe. Here, the amazing works on vitality in Yoruba culture by Margaret Thompson Drewal and Angela Roothan are relevant. These works are cited and engaged with by this element.

[2] Innocent Asouzu was among the early proponents of the view that the term 'anonymous African traditional philosophers' ought to stand as a placeholder for the originators/authors of the many traditional ideas and axiological frameworks that we know about in traditional African thought, whose names are lost to history.

(2020) have theorised about the meaning of life from the perspective of vitality. Furthermore, others like Agada (2020a) have used the concept of vitality to develop a proto-panpsychist vision of the world where vitality, reinterpreted as mood, is the fundamental component of all that exists.

Now, some controversies have, of course, emerged from discussions of vitality. In the first instance, scholars like Asouzu (2007b) and Matolino (2011) have questioned the intentions that undergird Tempels' attempt at articulating the Bantu conception of vitality. This intention, they claim, is racist, and if the idea is grounded in racism, then the view itself is inherently problematic. Related to this concern is the assumption of unanimity – the idea that all Africans believe the same thing – which has undermined African philosophies and worldviews, and inevitably led to the development of the more uncritical forms of ethnophilosophy that the 'Professional School' of African philosophy has so roundly criticised (Hountondji, 1996, p. 60). A third point of controversy has been the naturalisation of vitality by scholars like Metz, who view it as liveliness. While some have welcomed this move, there is criticism that liveliness disregards a fundamental aspect of vitality (that it is primarily religious and spiritual).

Like most ideas, the concept of vitality has emerged from a cultural, religious, and/or philosophical worldview and developed into a system of thought worthy of global engagement. Also, it has been applied in response to several philosophical problems (by advocates of vitality) and roundly criticised (by detractors and those who find it implausible). What this concise Element does is to present the reader with an overview of the notion of vitality in African philosophy of Religion, how the view has been applied by various scholars in different areas of African philosophy, as well as some of the problems that are associated with it. The Element also goes beyond mere description to offer a critical analysis of some of the ideas associated with vitality and provides the reader with the authors' unique views on the question of vitality.

It is in this way that this Element is significant. There is no Element or book-length material (as far as we know) that has systematically unpacked, addressed, and engaged various theories of vitality in the literature on African philosophy (of religion), explored how the notion of vitality addresses questions related to normative ethics, dignity and meaning in life, and crystallised some of the major criticisms of the view. Each of the sections of this Element either delineates the concept of vitality according to some traditions, speaks to various features of the concepts, or provides philosophical critiques of aspects of the view. And so, all the sections of this Element align with the current project of exploring an important concept in African philosophy of religion – the notion of vitality. Furthermore, we hope that this Element will also draw significant attention to the subject of vitality/vital force beyond the work of Tempels. Our goal is to offer a first step to understanding the various theories and core ideas of vitality by tracing its historical evolution and showing its contemporary continuity.

The Element comprises three main parts. Part I discusses some core ideas and theories of vitality within the context of the African philosophy of religion. The idea of vitality reflects much more than theorising the human body's functioning and establishing its material loci, such as the blood, brain, and breath. Within the traditional African philosophy of religion context, vitality repositions the relationship between human beings, the world, and non-living entities. By critically engaging with vitality in African philosophy of religion, we will show that the concept was deployed to unpack the complex, dynamic, and interwoven nature of existence.

In Part II of this Element, we examine how the notion of vitality has been articulated as a traditional African theory of ethics, navigating through meta-ethical problems such as the is/ought gap, as well as some of the views of some friends of the vitalist view. We describe one plausible theory of right action, according to the vitalist perspective, that sees right actions as follows: 'An action is morally acceptable insofar as it augments one's vitality, and an action is morally wrong insofar as it diminishes one's vitality (or the vitality of others), except in cases where self-defence is necessary.' Furthermore, we critically explore how African philosophers have rearticulated this notion of vitality as it pertains to ideas about dignity, focusing on a traditional conception of dignity that grounds dignity on the possession of the type of vitality that bears Godlike features such as consciousness, rationality, and so on, and the more contemporary liveliness view defended by scholars such as Metz. Finally, we examine the idea of vitality as a theory of meaning, focusing on the traditional views advocated by scholars like Mlungwana (2020) and Attoe (2020) and the proto-panpsychist/consolationist interpretation championed by Agada (2020b).

In Part III, we consider some criticisms that are often levelled (or might be levelled) against vitalist view(s). These criticisms range from the racial undertones that undergird the view to the claim that the more spiritualistic assumptions of the vitalist perspective are scientifically problematic, and Metz's critique that the naturalist views (and perhaps all current conceptions of vitality) are incapable of accounting for the value of progress and knowledge for its own sake.

Part I Some Core Ideas About the Nature of Vitality: Metaphysics and Religion

1 Vitality and Bantu Ontology

In this section, we will consider a key historical figure in the theorisation of the idea of vitality in African philosophy, Placide Tempels (1906–1977), a Belgian missionary who worked in the Belgian Congo (now the Democratic Republic of the Congo) during the colonial era. Tempels' book, titled *Bantu Philosophy*, originally published in Flemish but translated into English in 1959 has been crucial in articulating and systematising the notion of vitality in African philosophy through a reconstruction of the Bantu thought system that embodies the ideas, practices, and cultural worldview of the Baluba people with whom he had close encounters during his missionary work. Tempels believed that his efforts would help provide missionaries and colonialists acquire the proper lenses through which they could understand Bantu beliefs and practices and, in so doing, ease the burden of their so-called 'civilising mission' (see Tempels, 1959, pp. 19–20).

Indeed, Tempels criticises other fellow Europeans for their purely static outlook towards the ontological worldview of the Bantu people and, by extension, Africans. This static outlook viewed Africans as incapable of rational thought since, according to the view, Africans lacked the capacity for rationality. While the primitive and savage Africans were dehumanised and demonised, the so-called civilised European Christians were glorified. In response, Tempels argues that his fellow Europeans should imbibe a dynamic outlook that would be open to the ontological worldviews of others, such as the Bantu. He cautions that '[t]he gulf dividing Africans and Whites will remain and widen so long as we do not meet them in the wholesome aspirations of their own ontology' (Tempels, 1959, p. 18). Thus, for Tempels, it is by including African thought systems within the purview of what is taken to be a legitimate ontology that Europeans come to bridge the epistemic and social gaps between themselves and the African *other* and unveil the African as capable of some form of rational thought. Such unveiling, as E. Possoz (Tempels, 1959, pp. 11–12) notes in the book's preface, will force Europe to admit its 'ethnological mistake'[3] by recognising the rationality, logicality, and philosophy of Bantu ontology. One could, of course, argue that the belittling of African thought did not stem from any ethnological mistake but from a deliberate ideology that foregrounded the exploitation and exclusions of Africans, which will be a matter for another project. In any case, European colonisers (Tempels' audience) were largely averse to the African worldview and refused to approach it with any form of objectivity. And so, Tempels admonishes his audience to 'refrain from all such judgments (i.e., judgment upon the intrinsic worth of Bantu philosophy) keeping only to ethnology' and to 'understand Bantu philosophy, to know what their beliefs are and what is their rational interpretation of the nature of visible and

---

[3] Possoz attributes this ethnological mistake to the 'misunderstanding', 'fanaticism', and 'aversion' of Europeans towards Bantu ontology.

invisible things' (Tempels, 1959, p. 24). This move, for Tempels, will foster open-mindedness and the bracketing of all prejudices when approaching the African worldview, as well as the notion of vitality from the Bantu perspective.

In discussing the concept of vitality, we must bring our readers' attention to the fact that the concept is not exclusive to the Bantu or Africa. In fact, there is a significant body of literature in the West that engages vitality from scientific, biological, metaphysical, philosophical, and religious perspectives. We will not go into much detail and/or attempt to fully trace the history of the concept in European thought. But we must briefly mention the contributions of members of the Montpellier Medical School, especially in the mid-to-late eighteenth century, who proposed the vital force as a basic principle in living organisms (Haigh, 1985; Stollberg, 2000; Thornhill, 2020; Wolfe, 2022). Individuals like Paul-Joseph Barthez and Albrecht von Haller were among the early pioneers of this school. Barthez's 'vital principle' (see Haigh, 1977) and Haller's 'irritability and sensibility' account (see Cimino & Duchesneau, 1997) suggest that bodily activity and its organic function are independent of metaphysical properties like the soul. They describe bodily processes and functions as constitutive of the sort of animation propelled by vital force. Others like Georg Ernst Stahl [whose work on animism was brought to the Montpellier school by Francois Sauvages de Lacroix (see Thornhill, 2020)] consider bodily functions to be caused by a special metaphysical force referred to as the soul. The soul was taken to be a life-giving force created by God to animate living organisms. Furthermore, the presence of this special metaphysical force meant that a thing was alive, and its absence meant that it was inanimate/dead. By the last quarter of the nineteenth century to the early twentieth century, the idea of vitality had assumed a life of its own in the sciences, especially in the neo-vitalist works of Hans Driesch and Henri Bergson (see Spaulding, 1906; McLaughlin, 2003; Garrett, 2013; Bolduc 2023; Posteraro, 2023). They both believe that the life processes, growth, and evolution of living organisms cannot entirely be explained mechanistically. For instance, Driesch (1914) maintains that there is an immaterial causal entity responsible for the life processes, development, and evolution of living organisms, which he calls *entelechy*. He supports this with his empirical experiment with sea urchin embryos, where he observed that removing one of the four blastomeres (dividing cells) did not stop the cell from developing into a full organism. For him, this showed that there is an immaterial vital entity that guides and regulates the development of the sea urchin embryos. On his part, Bergson (2023) introduced the *élan vital* (vital impetus) as a force that drives life, creative evolution, and self-organization in living organisms.

With this massive body of literature on vitality in the West, one might question why Tempels introduced the concept of vital force in his book without referring to any of the existing works on the subject or why the view is often thought of as a *'peculiar trait of African philosophy and the cosmology which defines and shapes the framework within which the interwoven concepts of personhood and community, as extensions of Africa's concept of "being", are founded and reified'* (Italics original, Ngangah, 2019, p. 48). Furthermore, one might wonder whether Tempels' elucidation of the view was not an imposition of a popular philosophy in Western thought (at the time) on Bantu ontology. However, notwithstanding these questions, Tempels' interpretation and *exposition* of vital force within the African Bantu worldview, one can argue, added an African voice to the discussion and enriched the philosophical discourse on vitality.

In discussing the notion of vitality in Bantu ontology, Tempels points out that vitality plays a pivotal role in the lives of the Bantu people and their worldviews. As he puts it, ' … the key to Bantu thought is the idea of vital force … ' (Tempels, 1959, p. 33). In defining what is meant by the vital force,[4] a close reading of Tempels' work suggests that it is a non-physical (i.e., spiritual) and supra-sensible (i.e., not accessible to human empirical observation) principle that animates both living and non-living entities. Bantu ontology accounts for the processes and functions of living and non-living activities in terms of the indwelling activities of this vital force, which is spiritual and inaccessible to human empirical observations. Consider the following passages:

> Vital force is the reality which, though *invisible*, is supreme in man. Man can renew his vital force by tapping the strength of other creatures. (our italics, Tempels, 1959, p. 33).

And:

> Force, the potent life, [and] vital energy are the object of prayers and invocations to God, to the spirits and to the dead, as well as of all that is usually called magic, sorcery or magical remedies. The Bantu will tell you that they go to a diviner to learn the words of life, so that he can teach them the way of making life stronger. (Tempels, 1959, p. 31)

The above passages show the immateriality, empirical non-perceptibility, and near-inaccessibility of the vital force. Regardless of its immateriality, certain claims about the phenomenon can be made. If vitality is the embodiment of life and well-being (or a stronger life), and if it is true, as Tempels notes, that various

---

[4] Tempels uses a variety of terms to refer to vitality. These includes terms like 'force', 'life', 'life energy', 'life strength', 'life-force', 'vital energy', 'power', and 'being', etc. Tempels did not define any of these terms, which suggests that they mean the same thing, and African philosophers, in discussing vitality, have used these terms to refer to vitality (see, for instance, Okafor, 1982; Dzobo, 1992; Metz, 2012; Mlungwana, 2020).

types of activities can augment this vitality, then it would follow that all processes that allow for the increase or strengthening of one's vitality are desirable for a good life. This eventually culminates in what one might call the basic principle of Bantu ontology, which is that one ought to continually seek/pursue ways of increasing one's vital force, and one ought to refrain from anything that diminishes one's vital force.

For Tempels, the idea of force is the Bantu equivalent of the notion of being (although, in the dominant European view, force is only an attribute of being). While (for Tempels) the West has a static conception of being, the Bantu have a dynamic conception of being. That is, unlike the Europeans, who differentiate between being and force, the Bantu people make no such distinction. The Bantu, for Tempels, see force as being and not as an attribute of being. He writes:

> Herein is to be seen the fundamental difference between Western thought and that of the Bantu and other primitive people. (I compare only systems which have inspired widespread 'civilizations'). We can conceive the transcendental notion of 'being' by separating it from its attribute, 'Force', but the Bantu cannot. 'Force' in his thought is a necessary element in 'being', and the concept 'force' is inseparable from the definition of 'being'. There is no idea among Bantu of 'being' divorced from the idea of 'force'. Without the element 'force', 'being' cannot be conceived. (Tempels, 1959, p. 34)

In the above extract, Tempels holds that for the Bantu, being is force, not because it possesses force, for that will mean that force is an attribute of being, but because it is reality at the most fundamental level. This implies that the essence of all that exists is force. Tempels maintains that God, who is 'the Strong One', endows all living and non-living beings with vital force. Since vital force permeates all beings, the Bantu believe in the existence of 'divine force, celestial or terrestrial forces, human forces, animal forces, vegetable and even material or mineral forces' (Tempels, 1959, p. 35). In other words, Tempels holds that both animate and inanimate entities possess life force within Bantu ontology.

Now, some scholars like Patrick Aleke (2022, p. 10) are quick to dismiss the idea that inanimate objects possess some vitality. According to him, '[i]t would be ridiculous and at best strange to think that inanimate objects have life or vital force in African thought.' Aleke considers this view ridiculous because of Tempels' failure to demarcate between ontological force and vital force/the principle of life. As he argues, 'Definitely [inanimate objects] do have existential or ontological force, but not vital force. Existential or ontological force is the force that all beings (entities) have by the very fact that they do actually exist, while vital force is a superadded perfection that only animate things have.' He explains 'superadded perfection' as 'the qualities or properties that are possessed by particular kinds of beings, for instance, life for all living things, feeling for all sentient beings, and rationality or capacity for reasoning for rational beings' (Aleke, 2022, p. 10). While questions might be raised about the possibility of an overstretched interpretation of the Bantu view, some Contemporary African philosophers, like Agada (2020a, 2020b), following the proto-panpsychist perspective, have doubled down on the idea that all existent beings possess vitality, understood as a type of proto-mind that instantiates and animates being.

Extending the vitalist view even further, Tempels mentions that the varying levels of vital force that constitute an entity form an ontological hierarchy and determine that entity's place in that hierarchy. So, God, the Supreme being, occupies the top of the hierarchy of forces. This is followed by certain spiritual agents, such as the first archpatriarchs, who are the founding fathers of the various Bantu clans and to whom God first endowed the vital force. Then there are the dead who, in order of primogeniture, serve as a medium through which the archpatriarchal agents exert their influence on their living generations as a way of ensuring that vital force remains with their progeny. Next in the hierarchy are the living human beings, who are also stratified according to quantity and quality of vitality. After living humans, there is a category of lower forces, such as animals, vegetables, and minerals, which is also classified according to the quantity/quality of their vital power.

According to Tempels, vital energy is something that can be manipulated through various forms of interaction. This is especially true for conscious beings such as God, ancestors, and humans. For Tempels, this interaction of forces follows three immutable laws. The first law states that '[human beings] (living or deceased) can directly reinforce or diminish the being of another man. Such vital influence is possible from man to man.' The second law stipulates that '[t]he vital human force can directly influence inferior force beings (animal, vegetable, or mineral) in their being itself.' The third states that '[a] rational being (spirit, manes, or living) can act indirectly upon another rational being by communicating his vital influence to an inferior force (animal, vegetable, or mineral) through the intermediacy of which it influences the rational being' (Tempels, 1959, p. 45–46). From these laws, a few things are clear. First, the augmentation or diminution of an individual's vitality is dependent on how one interacts with other persons and the sorts of interactions that that individual receives from other rational agents. Second, it seems clear that beings at the higher end of the hierarchy of beings can directly influence the very essence (vitality) of beings at the lower end.

Finally, Tempels assures us (of the highly controversial claim) that the ontology of all 'primitive people', *all* Africans and all Bantu people, is based on this principle of vitality. This assumption of unanimity of African perspectives, what Asouzu calls the Tempelsian damage, has continued to be an unfortunate factor in how African philosophy is presented and how African philosophy is perceived. Also, if Tempels had been careful enough to admit that his vital force only mirrors the worldview of the Baluba/Bantu people, some of the criticism that trailed his philosophy would have been largely avoided (see Okafor, 1982; Hountondji, 1983; Matolino, 2011; Ogbonnaya, 2014). In his 'The Problem of "Man" in Bantu Philosophy', Kagame (1989) provides a different interpretation of being in Bantu philosophy. Basing his analysis on the Kinyarwanda language of the Rwandan people, he shows that the concept of being is integral to all cultures but linguistically expressed differently. He categorises Being into *muntu* (human being), *kintu* (things), *hantu* (place and time), and *kuntu* (modality). Kagame describes *Ntu* as the universal vital force manifesting and unifying these various categories of Being. Unlike Tempels, who generalised that his analysis of Bantu ontology represents the religious and philosophical beliefs of all 'primitive' Africans, Kagame makes it clear that his analysis centres on the worldview of the Rwandan people. However, Kagame has been criticised for being too Aristotelian in his interpretation of the view since he invested so much energy in attempting to prove that Aristotle's categories, like substance and relation, correlate with Bantu ontology (see Negedu, 2014; Roothan & Bello, 2024).

Paulin Hountondji has been vocal in his critique of Tempels' and Kagame's analysis of vitality in Bantu ontology. In a book chapter titled 'On African Philosophy' (1983), he describes both Tempels' and Kagame's Bantu philosophy as 'ethnophilosophy'. The designation of these two versions of Bantu philosophy as ethnophilosophy resulted from Tempels and Kagame seeking to excavate the supposed myths and folklore of the Bantu people and presenting the same as a legitimate philosophy seen as common to all Africans. In the words of Hountondji (1983, p. 22), Tempels' 'only weakness is that the philosophical form of [his] own discourse has been created in terms of a *myth* disguised as a collective philosophy.' Hountondji concludes that Bantu philosophy is nothing more than mythological thinking since it lacks the scientific rigour that is definitive of philosophy proper, and so cannot be passed on as such.

Others like Stephen O. Okafor (1982) and Matolino (2011) have criticised Tempels' Bantu philosophy as promoting the colonial agenda of racialism and the subjugation of Africans. For instance, Matolino argues that, first, Tempels' claim that Africans cannot engage in abstract metaphysical theorising and unpack their worldview philosophically is a refurbished version of the general enlightenment view that Africans are incapable of rational thought, as proposed by the likes of David Hume and Immanuel Kant (see More, 1996) and the views of anthropologists such as Lucien Levy-Bruhl (1926). Matolino calls this 'philosophical racialism' and argues that for Tempels to claim that the Bantu are ignorant of their worldview, he invented the word force to render Africans and their worldview in magical terms. Matolino also claims that Tempels' Bantu philosophy was aimed at aiding the colonial process (by providing a means of viewing the Bantu worldview – and, therefore, the mindset of the Bantu people) and providing some justification for the inferiorisation of Bantu people, by subtly questioning their ability to philosophise at the level of their European counterparts. We will say more about this criticism in Section 7.

Recently, Neils Weidtmann (2019) criticised Tempels for relying heavily on his Western Christian tradition to theorise vitality in Bantu philosophy. Notwithstanding this criticism, Weidtmann goes on to redefine vitality in relation to his interpretation of Ubuntu philosophy. While Ubuntu is often translated to mean 'humanness', Weidtmann rather takes it to 'refer to something like the generalization of vital force' (Weidtmann, 2019, p. 108). He bases his interpretation on the idea that the suffix '-*ntu*', in words like *muntu, ubuntu, bantu,* and so on, ' . . . literally means vital force' (Weidtmann, 2019, p. 108). Weidtmann (2019, p. 108) claims that the vital force 'must not be understood in the way Tempels . . . did but has to be seen in the context of experiencing the multidimensionality of human reality through a continuous revival of community at all levels'. Furthermore, for Weidtmann, vital force is neither the being of individuals nor their essence, as Tempels would have us believe.

However, Weidtmann is not particularly clear about what he means by 'experiencing the multidimensionality of human reality through a continuous revival of community at all levels' – a phrase he uses several times in his work – and how that sort of thing constitutes vitality. However, we interpret the phrase to mean the following: that for one to fully partake in all the possible dimensions of human experience, whether emotional, spiritual, rational, moral, physical, and so on, one must not only belong to a community but must also seek to enhance and rejuvenate that community. Consequently, one experiences vitality when one partakes in and enhances/rejuvenates the community.

This view of vitality, which is not explained further (at least ontologically) by Weidtmann, is not without problems. For instance, Weidtmann, at least in our interpretation of his view, takes vitality to be the experience and/or the recognition of a special type of well-being that comes with positively participating in a community. If true, then vitality is synonymous with the conditions that allow for the enhanced use of a human being's capacity to experience the world in a variety of ways. In other words, vitality would be consistent with human flourishing. If true, then the concept of vitality seemingly adds nothing to our understanding of the world, would be mostly redundant, and would seem like an arbitrary attachment of the term vitality to an already explained phenomenon since the proposed redefinition of vitality has already been captured in the literature by terms such as well-being (see Dzobo, 1992, Metz, 2012), flourishing, the joy of being (see Asouzu, 2004), and so on.

2 Vitality and the Concept of *Ase* in Yoruba Ontology

In this section, we will discuss vitality as it expresses itself in the Yoruba tradition, specifically in relation to the Yoruba concept of *ase*. In Yoruba thought, vitality is synonymous with the word *ase* (we will use both terms interchangeably, especially in this section), which literally means creative power, authority, and order. Others like P. R. McKenzie (1976, p. 191) have interpreted *ase* to mean a sort of 'secret and sacred power'. This interpretation of vitality or *ase* is based on a religious understanding of the concept. Our aim would be to reconceptualise *ase* and reveal its philosophical rendering while still drawing insights from its mystical/religious interpretation. We will also demonstrate that *ase* is a vital force and that the existence of things in the world is largely dependent on *ase* within the Yoruba worldview.

The first point to note is that *ase*, as vitality, is an all-pervading essence of all existent things. According to Margaret Thompson Drewal (1992, p. 27), *ase* is a 'generative Force or potential present in all things–rocks, hills, streams, mountains, plants, animals, ancestors, deities, humans–and utterances—prayers, songs, curses, and even everyday speech'. Similarly, Roland Abiodun (1994, p. 72, quoted from Vega, 1999 p. 46) defines *ase* as ' ... "power", "authority", "command", "sceptre"; [and as] the vital force in all living and non-living things; or coming to pass of an utterance, "a logos proforicos".' A few things are worthy of note from what has just been said. *Ase*, defined as power, generative force and/or potential, implicates the view that it is vitality, as an essential property, that forces being into existence. One could even say that it is vitality that instantiates being (see Agada, 2020b). As the seed of existence or life, vitality is necessarily inherent in all things, and all that exists must express vital energy through varying degrees of activity. Indeed, Henry John Drewal (N.D., online), Roland Abiodun (1994), and Nicole Mullen (2004) have argued that because of this vitality, no existent thing is lifeless and inanimate in the Yoruba worldview. Secondly, all existent things possess vitality, including God, divinities, spirits, ancestors, humans, animals, plants, stones, trees, gestures, songs, dances, rivers, and so on, and vitality is all-pervading because it is the very essence of existence, the primordial stuff from which things in the world emerge.

Furthermore, conscious instantiations of vitality, such as human beings, deities, and so on, can transcend mindless liveliness or activity and can manipulate the vital force itself. In this way, the vital force has intrinsic and instrumental value for conscious beings. Its intrinsic value lies in the conscious individual's very possession of vitality itself (as the essence of a thing and with the special property of consciousness). Its instrumental value lies in the capacity for good character or desirable activity (*iwa rere*) as a way of augmenting one's *ase*, as well as the active use of individuals' *ase* to realise their well-being and that of the community.

In discussions about *ase* in traditional Yoruba religion/ontology, one crucial question emerges, and this has to do with whether or not vitality reflects being at its most fundamental nature or whether it reflects a property of being. Recall that in Tempels' explanation of the vitalist view, he urged his readers to believe that, for the Bantu, being is synonymous with force. However, a problem arises when God is revealed to be a primordial being and the source of vitality (in which case, one might ask whether being – in particular, God – predates *ase*). This problem reveals itself when one considers traditional Yoruba cosmology.

In traditional Yoruba cosmology, there are two distinct but inseparable realms of existence: *Orun* (the non-physical/immaterial realm) and *aye* (the physical realm). Beings that exist in *Orun* are *Olorun* (God – also known by other cognate names such as *Olodumare, Eleda, Eleemi*), etc.), *Orisa* (divinities), *oro, iwin, ajogun,* and *eghe (*spirits), and *ara orun* (ancestors) –all of which possess *ase* in varying degrees.

Olorun, God, is the possessor of *ase*. *Olorun* is also the source of *ase* and is considered to be a necessary being. This means that *Olorun* necessarily exists and cannot fail to exist. As a necessary being, *Olorun* is the foundation of the cosmos. In other words, all that exist take their token of existence from (and are dependent on) *Olorun*. These are all very interesting claims that the reader must bear in mind, as they lead to a variety of possibilities regarding the nature of *ase*. In the first instance, *Olorun* might be interpreted as a necessary and primordial entity that is responsible for the emergence of the vital force. This view is sustained and supported by the fact that God is seen as an entity that also has some sort of personality, with intentions and goals. This latter fact suggests that God is a being that is separate from pure vitality because if pure vitality reflected consciousness, personality, rationality, and so on, then all entities, including inanimate entities, would reflect these specific Godlike features (since all that exists expresses vitality). If God is separate from vitality in this way, then it must be the case that vital force is not synonymous with being since vitality is not, according to this view, synonymous with God. Thus, according to this reading, it would be true that in Yoruba metaphysics, *ase* is merely an important attribute of being.

In the second instance, one could say that *Olorun* is *an embodiment* of vitality, not unlike other instantiations of vitality (other existent things), but also the purest manifestation, embodiment/instantiation of vitality. This interpretation may seem contrary to the view that God is the *source* of vitality, but if one reflects on God as a *necessary embodiment* of vitality, then that contrariness fades away. Furthermore, God as the source of vitality might only reflect the idea that other instantiations of vitality only spring into existence because of the existence of the vital force, which God necessarily embodies. God, being conscious, might instantiate itself in varying degrees, thus creating the hierarchy of beings that is based on what instantiation of God best reflects the Godlike properties of consciousness, personality, rationality, and so on, properties that are also all essential to God's nature.[5] This view, which can be interpreted as a form of pantheism (although some might argue that it is a type of panentheism), would also align with the alleged intuitions of the Bantu that being *is* force.

There is a third possible interpretation that might view *ase* as a primordial force, which is just as necessary as *Olorun* but also a *property* of God. In the creation of other beings – Yoruba cosmology posits that *Olorun works* with the *Orisa* (other lower divinities) to create the world (see Idowu, 1962; Abimbola, 2006; Fayemi, 2007). Olorun imbues all created beings with this Godlike property in varying degrees. While it is hard to know if *ase* is an *essential* property of God, one could argue that *ase* is an essential/fundamental property for other created things.

Beyond all these arguments, some scholars, like Emmanuel Ofuasia (2024), take substance metaphysics as a poor lens through which to view African/Yoruba metaphysics. In this way, thinking of *ase* as some static essential property on which some accidental properties inhere might reflect an undue imposition of Aristotelian-type metaphysics on an African worldview. Thus, a more dynamic/process/event-based interpretation would be important, where *ase* is an ever-evolving thing that instantiates itself in various ways across time. According to this sort of thinking, *Olorun* and all else that exists are all expressions of an ever-evolving vitality. *Olorun* would thus be subject to *ase* and not prior to it (similar to our second interpretation above).

---

[5] To be sure, the argument for consciousness, rationality, personality, etc., as Godlike properties goes like this: God is the essence – or perhaps embodiment – of vitality. God is also presumably conscious and intrinsically moral (perhaps, also immoral). God also imbues all that exists with vitality in varying degrees. Unlike other biological life and non-living things, human vitality has the special quality of consciousness, which is taken to special. Thus, unlike animals and non-living things, only humans, ancestors, and/or spirits (who are imbued with this property by God) have this special property that only God (originally) possesses. Furthermore, if consciousness is essential to the nature of God (the vitalist, at least from what can be gleaned in the literature, would not accept an unconscious and depersonalised God), and humans possess this quality, albeit to a lesser degree, then humans possess a Godlike property.

Despite the variety of arguments provided in this section, one thing that seems clear in the literature is the view that *Olorun* possesses *ase* in some way, and *Olorun* is responsible for the presence of *ase* in everything that exists (Drewal, 1992; Abiodun, 1994; Hallgren, 1995; Mullen, 2004; Roothan & Bello, 2024).

The dominant traditional Yoruba view suggests that *Olorun* endows all entities in *Aye* with *ase*. *Aye* is the physical realm and the realm of contingent things in which entities come into and go out of existence. These entities that exist in the physical realm include visible and material entities encountered in everyday life, such as human bodies, stones, trees, land, and so on. *Ase* flows through all contingent existence, breathes life into *Aye*, and sustains it.

The nature of *Olorun's* relationship with *Aye* has been explained in a variety of ways, and the extent to which *Olorun* interferes with the affairs of other creatures in *Aye* has been hotly debated. Two kinds of explanation have assumed some degree of prominence in Yoruba metaphysics. The first one is the idea that *Olorun* is present in *Aye*. There are two versions of this idea in the literature. The first version rests on monotheism, which is championed by scholars like Bolaji Idowu (1962), Adebowale Akintola (1999), Omotade Adegbindin (2011), and Oyeshile (2021). Utilising resources from the monotheistic Christian tradition of the West, Idowu (1962, p. 204) developed a form of 'diffused monotheism' that recognises *Olorun* as the ultimate controlling power and works with other divinities to maintain order in *Aye*. Oyeshile (2021, p. 4) explains that '[t]he Yoruba trace their source to the Supreme Being because they believe that human existence has both natural and supernatural sources, giving precedence to the latter and seen [sic] the former as being dependent on the supernatural.' Here, all entities in *Aye* seem to be dependent on *Olorun* for their sustenance without *Olorun* depending on them. That is, all entities in *Aye* need *Olorun* in order to exist and survive, while *Olorun* necessarily exists without depending on any of these entities. The other version leans towards panentheism, of which scholars like Ofuasia (2020) are major proponents. In his process panentheism, Ofuasia builds on Alfred North Whitehead's process metaphysics. In Ofuasia's view, *Olorun* and *Aye* are distinct entities, but both are actually and ontologically the same, thereby avoiding dualism and diffused monotheism. Since they are ontologically the same, both *Olorun* and *Aye* fundamentally share the same existence: *Olorun* being in *Aye* and *Aye* being in *Olorun,* regardless of their differences. God as an actual entity constitutes two aspects: mental/abstract and physical/concrete states, which makes them dipolar. He affirms that, through this dipolar state, ' . . . the world depends on God' and 'God also depends on the world' in Yoruba metaphysics (Ofuasia, 2020, p. 53).

The *Olorun-Aye* interaction is interwoven in a web of relationships, involving a relationship of mutual dependence. This shows that *Olorun* is greatly present in *Aye* and very much actively involved in the events in *Aye*, and interferes with the affairs of the world and vice versa. The second explanation, which is a reaction to the first one, is that *Olorun* is detached from *Aye*. This explanation is closely related to deism, in which God created the world and then became distant from it. Drewal, Pemberton III, and Abiodun (1989, p. 14) uphold this position when they claim that *Olorun* is 'conceived as the creator of existence ... and generally distant, removed from the affairs of both divine and world beings.' They believe that after *Olorun* created *Aye, Olorun* allowed it to operate without interfering. They claim that while other divinities, spirits and ancestors interfere with Aye, *Olorun* stays away. Each of these explanations has advantages and disadvantages worthy of philosophical engagement, which unfortunately will not be done here. But it is worth noting that the Yoruba religious/metaphysical worldview strongly affirms the presence of *ase* in the world without *Olorun* and *Aye* losing their distinct identity.

We now explore how *ase* expresses itself in human beings. For the Yoruba, the nature of the human being is characterised by the presence of *ase*, which is connected to the ultimate realities of *Orun* and *Olorun*. *Ase* in humans is equated with *emi*, which signifies the life-giving property/entity. However, there is controversy in Yoruba ontology on how *emi* should be translated into the English language. Scholars like Wande Abimbola (1971), Akin Makinde (1984), Babatunde Lawal (2005), Oyelakin Taye (2013), and Akinola Akomolefe (2016) claim that *emi* should be translated as 'soul' – a purely immaterial, spiritual, and invisible entity animating the human body. Makinde (1984, pp. 191–192) establishes that '*emi*, the real thing that gives a body its life, is not subject to destruction by human beings precisely because it is not moulded out of physical substance but a spiritual gift from Olodumare [Olorun] – a divine breath of Olodumare himself.' He concludes that 'the soul, like its creator, never dies; this is why we talk of "dead bodies" but never of "dead souls". Rather, it deserts its temporary earthly abode – the mortal body – and goes back to its creator, *Olodumare* (God) in heaven.' In this sense, *emi* is also the divine spark in humans and the imperishable and indestructible element that does not die when an individual dies but returns to *Orun*, where it becomes an ancestor.

Other scholars like Olufemi Morakinyo and Akinsola Akiwowo (1981), Barry Hallen and Sodipo (1986), Segun Gbadegesin (2004), and Oladele Balogun (2007) disagree with the translation of *emi* as soul and insist that it is a vital force or life-force or life breath. According to Morakinyo and Akiwowo:

> *Emi* ... seems to have been mistranslated by previous writers who have given it the connotation of 'ghost' or 'soul.' When the use of the word *emi* is examined more closely, the best equivalent that can be coined in the English language is 'life-force.' Every living thing has *emi* [that] enables it to continue living. (Morakinyo & Akiwowo, 1981, p. 27)

This implies that *emi*, as life force, is what activates the body (*ara*), without which the body will be lifeless (and it is *Olorun* that supplies the body with life). Clearly, this controversy is not about whether *emi* exists as part of human makeup but how it should be translated. Delving into this controversy in detail, although philosophically worthwhile, will be a great digression. One thing we can glean from this controversy is that humans possess a life principle, be it soul or life force, that powers and energises the body.

The Cyclic Transference of Ase

Another important idea in the Yoruba conception of vitality is the cyclic transference of *ase* or vitality (see Figure 1).

In the diagram in Figure 1, Ase_0 symbolises the non-physical world (*Orun*), the spiritual realm of existence that includes *Olorun* (the creator and source of *ase*) and other deities, spirits, and ancestors. Ase_1 represents the physical world that comprises the material realm of existence, which includes, among other entities, humans whom *Olorun* endows with *ase*. Ase_{-1} signifies the dead loved ones transitioning to the realm of *Orun* to become ancestors, and/or where they await to be reborn. Furthermore, Ase_0 are necessary beings who cannot fail to exist; Ase_1 are contingent beings who live, die, and reincarnate; Ase_{-1} are ancestral beings, and Ase_{+1} are merely possible beings that do not exist but could exist, for instance, through reincarnation. The diagram shows the cyclic process in which human existence unfolds as the self-actualisation of *ase*. This cyclic process is the continual drive of *ase* toward self-transcendence. While Ase_0 permeates all existence, it actualises self-transcendence through human lives and activities. Once humans have lived the number of years assigned to them by *Olorun*, they die and carry back their Ase_{-1} to *Olorun*, and they will be reborn as a child endowed with some portion of their *ase* (Ase_{+1}), and this process is continuous. The cyclical nature of *ase* is the belief that *ase manifests itself* as/through *Aye* and

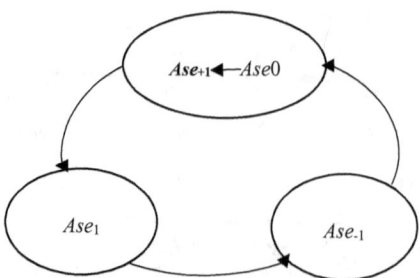

Figure 1 A diagram of the cyclic transference of *ase*

returns to *Orun* in a cyclic motion, and humans play their role in this process through a protracted struggle of nurturing and growing one's *ase*.

Humans can develop, nurture, and grow their *ase*. As Angela Roothan and Saheed A. Bello (2024, p. 68) put it, *ase* is 'developed, nurtured, and activated through personal/life experiences and the ontological journey of Yoruba ritual and cosmology.' Positive life and religious experiences (rituals, divinations, and worship), including the fulfilment of one's destiny (*ori*) enhance one's *ase* in much the same way that negative experiences tarnish one's *ase*.

The communal components to nurturing and growing one's *ase* involve the active and positive use of one's vitality. Even though *ase* is something that individuals have by virtue of being born, they must play an active role through their actions to nurture and grow it. The Yoruba believe that individuals progressively nurture their *ase* as they participate in ongoing communal relationships by fulfilling their obligations and duties. The proper use of one's *ase* involves contributing to the general well-being of the community. This communal component of nurturing and growing one's *ase* is tied to individual *iwa* (character), and one's current *iwa* impacts one's life circumstance as well as the future possibilities of being an ancestor and being reborn. For instance, *Iwa rere* (good character) leads to good circumstances in life and increases the likelihood of one becoming an ancestor. On the contrary, *iwa buburu* (bad character) leads to unfortunate circumstances in life (see Ofuasia, 2024). According to Drewal, '[i]f one makes positive contributions during one's life, a portion of the person's performative power or being (*ase*) may come back again as a new individual with a new spiritual head or destiny' (Drewal, Online, p. 215).

Since reincarnation is possible (see Idowu, 1962; Awolalu & Dopamu, 2005), the cyclic process of *ase* allows humans the opportunity to develop their *ase* by performing morally good actions that build character throughout each birth and making spiritual efforts to become an ancestor and possibly reincarnate (see Fig. 1). The Yoruba often refer to those who have developed and nurtured their *ase* as *Alaase*. They include diviners, queens, priests, kings, masqueraders, and so on. (see Drewal, Pemberton III, & Abiodun, 1989).

From a wider metaphysical perspective, one way that the theological perspectives of the Yoruba, as they relate to *ase,* can be interpreted is by thinking about the view as a metaphor for a grander philosophical point. One can, for instance, view the *Orun* and *aye*, as representative of the dual but complementary nature of *ase* as a primordial being that is both physical and non-physical and capable of instantiating itself as such. In Yoruba metaphysics, all beings possess an *ori* or destiny, which they must fulfil, and this idea can be interpreted to show that an ever-evolving *ase* instantiates various entities in a *determined* variety of ways. In other words, from the cosmic perspective, the striving of human beings to fulfil their destiny only reflects the unfolding of human beings as instances of *ase*. Destiny, in this sense, is nothing more than the predetermined process of the unfolding of the individual as one instance of *ase*.

Furthermore, the cyclic transference of *ase*, described in this section, can be understood to reflect the ever-changing nature of the various instantiations of *ase*, as they manifest themselves as a physical entity, as an immaterial entity, and as *ase* in its purest form. Thus, one can conceive of *ase* as *being qua being*, and all that we know to exist are purely instances or a specific manifestation of *ase*. According to this interpretation, *ase* is not a property of being and is not (technically) an all-pervading energy. It is rather being itself.

Now, there is one small controversy that friends of the traditional vitalist view (including the Bantu and Yoruba view) ought to deal with in order to avoid contradictions with the above view. The first is the more serious problem. Recall that earlier, we mentioned that, according to the Bantu ontology, the diminution of the vital force is what constitutes immorality or a lack of well-being, finally to the point of death. In other words, it is taken for granted that the total diminution of the vital force in the human being causes death. If this is true, then what are we to make of the claim that at death, the individual's vital force re-congregates, once again, at the non-physical realm (either to re-emerge as an ancestor or to return to God)? If the total loss of vitality brings death, what then returns to God or becomes an ancestor?

This problem is not well dealt with in the Bantu view,[6] but our current interpretation of the Yoruba view can provide us with a plausible response. It could very well be true that various manifestations of *ase* interact with each other in various ways. And it might very well be true that certain forms of interactions (negative interactions) might cause a particular instantiation of *ase* to cease to be (what one might call death). Still, death, in this view, would not mean a total loss of vitality (in the sense that one's vitality ceases to exist) but rather (1) a recession of *ase* into its purest form and/or (2) re-instantiation of *ase* in other forms (physical and/or spiritual). In other words, certain forms of interaction can force an instance of *ase* to recede from its specific manifestation back to its original form (or, perhaps, manifest in other ways), or those interactions might force an instance of *ase* to re-instantiate itself as a specific physical (say a dead body) and/or immaterial entity (say as some sort of spiritual agent). Through the interaction between various instances of *ase*, the transference of *ase* from instance A to instance B can also result in (1) and (2) for A and B, or even the enhancement of B.

---

[6] One could interpret the Bantu view as suggesting that the experience or perpetration of evil, as a mode of reducing vitality, does not mean a loss (disappearance) of vital energy but a sort of slow return of parts of one's vitality back to the supreme being.

3 Vitality and *'Ndu'* in Igbo Ontology

In this section, we present and critically examine the idea of vitality from the Igbo religious/philosophical context. The first concept that immediately comes to the fore in the Igbo conception of vitality is the concept of *ndu,* which is etymologically interpreted as 'life'. According to Elochukwu Uzukwu (1982, p. 195), '*ndu* is a noun meaning life, existence, being. The verb *di* or *du* means to be, to exist (to be alive).'

Now, there are a few things to note following what we have said so far. If *ndu* or life expresses *being-becoming* [as Anyanwu (1984, p. 74) notes] and at the same time expresses vitality, then it must be the case that existing is synonymous with vitality, and for a thing to exist at all in the world, it must possess vitality. If *ndu* is described in this way, then vitality is essential to being since it is the very thing that instantiates being in the world. In other words, both existence and vitality (which we take to be synonymous) point not merely to a static property of being but to the *capacity to be* in its most fundamental form, which is not static, and for which the different things in the world are merely instances or expressions of that capacity. *Ndu* as the *capacity to be* is itself expressive of this capacity and so manifests itself as a fundamental reality that is necessary and constantly becoming, for if it brings life to being(s) as we know them (that is, if it is responsible for projecting being to the world and to the conscious mind), and if *ndu* is the *capacity to be* then it makes sense to think of this pure capacity to exist as, itself, an embodiment of existence. For if it were not an existing thing (or better put, the embodiment of existence itself), then it could not do the job of instantiating/projecting the variety of things we perceive into existence. This might sound slightly tautologous, but there is no better way of explaining the view.

As the *capacity to be*, *ndu* is present in all reality. This is what Uzukwu means when he insists that *ndu* "stands out for the Igbo as a value around which other values find their meaning. *Ndubuisi* (life is first), *ndukaku* (life is greater than wealth) are proper names pregnant with meaning" (Uzukwu, 1982, p. 195). Perhaps the word 'pervade' does not properly capture what we mean, but an illustration might help. Things in the world are markedly different – a stone is, for instance, different from a person – but different things have in common the fact that they exist because of *ndu*. In fact, one can conclude that these things are specific instances of *ndu* manifested in various compelling ways. So, when K. C. Anyanwu (1984, p. 90) says that '[f]or the Igbo, everything in the universe is alive or a life-force, that is, life-force or life is what every experienced reality possesses', we do not interpret him to mean that even non-living things are animate and possess some sort of mentality (although one can very much argue that this is the case). What we interpret the claim to mean is that the very thing that presents a thing as an existent thing in the world is *ndu*. Life or life force, here, does not merely mean animation but something more – the inherent capacity of a thing to be present in the world. Thinking of *ndu* in this way showcases it as something that is inherently and intrinsically valuable since it is the very thing that allows things to manifest themselves as existent things. In a way, existent things are synonymous with *ndu,* or are an instantiation of it, since nothing exists without *ndu* – in other words, we cannot think of anything separate from *ndu* because every component of that thing exists because of *ndu*.

One important point to note in all this is the idea that the way objects in the world manifest reflects a capacity that is already present in *ndu*. Living things, for instance, are seemingly animate, and so the capacity for animation is already present in *ndu*.

For the traditional Igbo philosophers, the human being is seen as a manifestation of goodness and beauty, which is also inherent in *ndu*. This thinking can be derived from a linguistic analysis of the Igbo description of the human person as *mmadu*. In one interpretation of the term, Jonathan Chimakonam and Lucky Ogbonnaya define it (from their understanding of its etymology) as '"*muo di ndu*" (the spirit that is alive and can be touched)' (Chimakonam & Ogbonnaya 2015, p. 278). This definition establishes the human being as a particular kind of physical instantiation of *ndu*. The human being is not merely a physical being but a spiritual thing in physical form. Indeed, the human being is seen as a prime example of the conscious expression of the intertwining of the spiritual and the physical. *Mmadu*, in this case, serves as a vital link between entities in *uwa mmadu* (the realm of physical reality) and *uwa mmuo* (the realm of spiritual reality). As a vital link, human beings are in a relationship with other spiritual entities such as God (*Chi/Chukwu*), ancestors, spirits, nature, and their fellow humans. And since life is the ultimate reality, humans become aware of this relationship as they go on to live or experience life. This sort of thinking plays into the general vitalist understanding of the human being as essentially vital force and animated by a vital force.

In another interpretation, some scholars like Raymond Arazu (1978), Uzukwu (1982), and Emmanuel Edeh (1985), believe that *mmadu* (sometimes referred to as *mmadi*) means let beauty/goodness be/exist. Others like Okafor (1982), Andrew I. Isiguzo, George Ukagba, and Nkeonye Otakpor (2004), and Udobata Onunwa (2012) disagree. For Isiguzo, Ukagba, and Otakpor (2004), *Mmadu* literally means the beauty/goodness/crown point of life. These two interpretations, though very similar, are slightly different. In the first interpretation, as in the second, there is an indication that the *ndu* that projects the human being in the world has an inherent goodness/beauty. But, admittedly, it is unclear if this goodness or beauty is intrinsic or externally observed. Perhaps one can conclude that inherent in *ndu* (as the capacity to be) is also the capacity to be good or bad, and this capacity relies on the idea that relationships between instantiated things might be beneficial or detrimental, depending on context. In terms of differences, one gets the sense that in the first interpretation, the goodness or beauty of the human being is in *process*. In other words, the way in which *ndu* is instantiated in the human being projects a potential for special goodness or beauty. This interpretation is supported by the various normative conceptions of personhood (both radical and moderate) that we find in the literature on African philosophy. In the second interpretation, the thinking seems to be that the human being, as a special manifestation of *ndu*, is inherently beautiful and good. This goodness or beauty, as we understand it, is more aesthetic than it is moral. Either way, both interpretations gesture to the fact that the *ndu* that instantiates the human being is of a special kind. This is also why human life, within the Igbo worldview, is of 'supreme value' (see Uzukwu, 1982, p. 203; Anyanwu, 1984, p. 100).

There are some, like Obiajulu Ibeabuchi (2013), who, like Tempels, believe that the life force in human beings (referred to as '*Obi*' in Ibeabuchi's work) can be increased or diminished depending on the performance of certain activities. Indeed, Ibeabuchi believes that, in the Igbo worldview, humans can strengthen their *obi/ndu/*vitality through certain rituals or by living a good life. Conversely, living a bad life, as well as the interference of some other life forces, such as witches and unappeased deities, could diminish individuals' *obi*. The similarities between the views expressed by Ibeabuchi and Tempels are uncanny, and one wonders whether the former's view is not a product of the strong influence of Tempels' view.[7] However, if it is the case that vitality is legitimately understood in this way within the traditional Igbo metaphysical worldview, then we can interpret the augmentation or diminution of vitality as a product of the interaction of the various instantiations of *ndu/obi,* and we can agree that an increase or reduction of *ndu/obi* results in a change in the very nature of a (human) being. In this way, a reduction in vital force reduces the capacity of the human being to remain an instance of a human being, and an increase in vitality may not only entrench the human being as a strong instance of a human being but might also lead to some sort of transcendence. In other words, the weaker one's vitality, the higher the chances that the individual ceases to remain

---

[7] Scolars like Francis Njoku (2002), Asouzu (2011), and Charles Ikechukuwu Okoro and Christian C. Emedolu (2020) argue that Tempels' theory of vitality in Bantu ontology has had an undue influence on African scholars who sought to understand this vital force in the Igbo worldview, and that how vitality is understood in the Igbo view is somewhat dissimilar to Tempels' view. This is part of what Asouzu (2007) has described as the Tempelsian damage.

a human being, or an existent thing. The stronger one's vitality, the more vibrant the individual becomes. And it is further possible for such persons with very high levels of vitality to transcend normal human capacities (examples would be diviners, priests, etc.).

Despite this criticism, we believe that the concept of vitality in Igbo ontology has some merits. *Ndu*, as the universal life-force, is celebrated through its active presence in humans and humans' direct participation in it. This has positioned humans at the centre of the universe and as a life-force interacting with other life-forces with which they form an organic whole. This organic whole is sustained by *ndu* and apprehended as humans experience life.

Part II Vitalist Approaches in African Philosophy of Religion

4 Vitality and Ethics

Some Meta-ethical Considerations

From the religious and metaphysical outlines of the vitalist view in Part I, we examine how the vitalist view manifests itself as an ethical theory. The main idea of a vitalist theory of ethics is the view that morality resides in augmenting vitality in oneself and others – we will explain this point later in this section. However, we begin by stating the main thesis of the vitalist theory of ethics because this thesis allows us to tackle some questions before the view can be properly articulated. The questions we have in mind are interrelated meta-ethical questions. The first question is one that Molefe (2022) has already asked, which can be restructured in this way: if we take the vital force (or the augmenting of it) to be the signpost for what morality entails, then we must ask whether moral properties can be supernatural or not. The second question, which we must also deal with, is the question of whether a metaphysical notion of a state of affairs (an increase or decrease in vital force) generally implies a normative view (that one ought to increase their vitality, as this is a moral thing to do), and, if so, how? This second question basically points to the is/ought gap problem.

Regarding the first question, we must first take for granted that something like the vital force does exist in the way that some traditional vitalists (such as the anonymous traditional Bantu, Yoruba, and Igbo philosophers and others who take their views seriously) believe it to exist. Then, we must ask about the nature of moral properties. The idea that moral properties, like rightness and wrongness, can be supernatural may not be new. In Judeo-Christian traditions, there is the suggestion that God's commands are the essence of rightness and wrongness. This word of God, or command of God, has a spiritual nature and potency since God, the source of this word, is presumably spiritual. While Divine command is fairly straightforward in its nature – it is spiritual and prescriptive – vitality or vital force is something different. Metaphysically speaking, vitality reveals itself as something spiritual (as per the traditional view) and something that originates from the Supreme being, who stands as its source and the very embodiment of vitality. If we take this to be true, then it is easy to take vitality to be a spiritual thing. The problem arises when we ask whether vitality is inherently normative (in the way that God's commands are normative), and here it gets tricky. On the face of it, there is nothing moral or normative about vital force qua vital force, and, if true, then it would be false to claim that vitality embodies the notions of rightness or wrongness in a way that having more or less vitality equals being more or less moral. Nevertheless, it is possible for vitalists to arm-twist the view to conform to the disputed notion. One can, for instance, appeal to the idea that God is essentially a moral being (all-good,[8] perhaps) and that the essential metaphysical component of God is the vital force. If both claims are true, then there are good grounds to ground God's normative essence on Its[9] spiritual essence – there must be something about vitality, as an essential characteristic of God, that makes God essentially good or moral. It is the same way that reductionists, in discussions about the mind, can insist that there is something about the brain that makes it the seat of consciousness, such that one cannot divorce a functioning/living brain from a conscious mind. If this is true, and if it is true that this essential component of God is infused in the human being, then one can also conclude that having more or less of this vitality would mean being more or less good (or Godlike), and that this is where the (moral) value of vitality lies. Indeed, Pantaleon Iroegbu, cited by Molefe (2018, p. 25), notes that life (vital force) is valuable 'because it is divine in resemblance, it must be taken loftily and with the highest respect. It must be seen for what it is: of high value.' Many traditionalists would probably agree with this move.

Another move would be to deny that vitality constitutes moral property and claim that we must think of morality and vitality in relational ways. If one takes vitality to be a bare metaphysical item, bearing no normative parts, and also takes the possession of more or less vitality to increase or decrease our ability to live life with more verve and vigour, then we can conclude that having more or less vitality makes an individual's life more or less good, enjoyable or worth living (see Lougheed, Molefe, & Metz, 2024). It is the same way that one would

---

[8] It is important to note that in some African religious/philosophical traditions, God is not all good, and is fairly limited.
[9] We describe God as an It, since nothing definitively proves God to be gendered or that God favours one gendered description over the other (see Attoe, 2022).

conclude that having good health, as opposed to bad health, is good for the individual, all things being equal. Now, while having more or less vitality might be good for the individual, we are not necessarily talking about a moral good. However, since having more vitality engenders a good life, it would seem (morally) right to, at the very least, help others obtain more vitality rather than undermine their achievement of vitality, which would be morally wrong. This is especially true from a complementary perspective, where the well-being of others is necessary for the well-being of the individual. A high degree of vitality then becomes an object – a final good – that is worth pursuing for its own sake and an object that demands a dutiful (which can be construed as a moral duty) pursuit. This duty to pursue and sustain a high degree of vitality is also a duty to help others attain this final good. So, the properties of right and wrong, as well as the associated duties, lie firmly on the vital force as a final good that is worth pursuing. Thus, a life with more vitality has achieved some goodness, aided others in achieving this goodness, or both. The amount of vitality one has, thus, becomes a badge of recognition for one's morality and something worth pursuing. This move would likely appeal to both traditionalists and contemporary liveliness theorists.

This brings us to the is/ought gap or fallacy, which seeks to decipher how exactly descriptive/metaphysical claims can suddenly become normative and prescriptive. Within our subject matter, the question becomes how the claim 'human beings possess vitality' translates to the claim 'it is morally right for human beings to augment their vitality'. To answer this question requires us to provide a bridge premise that links both claims together, and here, our discussion in the previous two paragraphs might help. From what we said in this section, two bridge premises are possible. The first possible premise tugs on the idea that the vital force could be, by its metaphysical nature, inherently moral. By claiming that God is essentially moral and that the vital force captures that essentiality, one could say that vitality is the actual metaphysical expression of morality. If we add the fact that no vitality implies death, we arrive at our bridge premise:

a. Human beings possess vitality;
b. *Vitality is a direct expression of morality*;
c. Therefore, it is morally right for human beings to augment their (and others') vitality, and it is immoral for human beings to engender the loss of vitality in themselves and others.

The second possible bridge premise is based on the idea that possessing more vitality is a final good worth pursuing. If this is true and if vitality is an essential component of the individual (such that little or no vitality implies suffering and death), then pursuing this good is something worth doing. In the same vein, deliberately causing other people to suffer the loss of this good would not be a worthwhile endeavour. This is why scholars like Molefe have drawn this distinction between maximising life and securing death as opposites that express moral goodness and moral badness (the 'worst moral evil', as he puts it), respectively (Molefe, 2022, p. 23). The pursuit and undermining of this final good must have moral consequences. Thus, we could include a bridge premise as follows:

a. Human beings possess vitality;
b. *Vitality is a final good that is worth possessing*;
c. Therefore, it is morally right for human beings to augment their (and others') vitality, and it is immoral for human beings to engender the loss of vitality in themselves and others.

Now, one might find various arguments against these viewpoints, and those criticisms may or may not be worthwhile. However, what we have done here so far is attempt to address some important meta-ethical questions by proffering possible responses that are based on our current understanding of the vitalist views. These responses allow us to move forward as we try to discuss vitality as a proper ethical theory.

The Ethics of Vitality: The Traditional[10] Religious View

For scholars like Molefe (2022, p. 23), there are three ways in which the vitalist view can be interpreted as a normative theory, viz. 'a consequentialist, deontological and a perfectionist interpretation [or rendition] of vitality', From a consequentialist perspective, what is of paramount concern for the vitalist is the question of what actions maximise or diminish vitality. In other words, the morality of an action depends on how much that action increases the vitality of both the moral agent and the moral patient. Molefe further states that while vitality is deontologically accounted for 'in terms of actions that honour vitality, a perfectionist interpretation accounts for permissible actions in terms of those actions that perfect one's character, by way of acquiring more vitality' (Molefe, 2022, p. 24).

Our approach here, however, is to respond to the following question: What would stand as a viable principle of right action from a vitalist standpoint based

---

[10] We take traditional to mean a version of vitality that purports to appeal to some cultural worldview (say the Bantu view, or the Yoruba view), as opposed to versions of the view that have been significantly reconstructed by individual philosophers.

on what we already know of the view from the available ideas in the literature? Our response to this question is as follows:

> *An action is morally acceptable insofar as it augments one's vitality, and an action is wrong insofar as it diminishes one's vitality.*

To properly understand this view, it is important to discuss some of its relevant metaphysical underpinnings. When we say that morality involves the augmentation of one's vitality or that immorality involves activities that undermine/diminish vitality, recourse must be made to the sort of activities or states of affairs that metaphysically warrant an exhibition of vitality. Metz (2012, p. 25) identifies some of these to include 'a superlative degree of health, strength, growth, reproduction, creativity, vibrancy, activity, self-motion, courage and confidence ... ' as activities that exhibit vitality, while 'disease, weakness, decay, barrenness, destruction, lethargy, passivity, submission, insecurity and depression', (one can add death), and so on, are the sort of things that not just fail to exhibit but also diminish vitality. Indeed, one can crystallise and categorise the above into activities that ensure that life goes well and activities that undermine individual well-being.

It is worth noting that because humans are social beings and because these ideas are steeped in deeply relational metaphysics, activities that express vitality are *not* the sort of activities that exhibit false self-interestedness.[11] Thus, cunning (especially the type that undermines the well-being of others) and any activity that undermines other people for the sake of attempting to make one's own life go well are morally bad actions. One exception could be something like a just or necessary war. Although war in itself can be viewed as bad since it means that the lives of many participants would not go well (by virtue of injury, death, mental health problems, etc.), where the absence of war implies the diminishing of even more vitality, then war would, at least, be permissible. However, to avoid loopholes that would permit things like arbitrarily killing a patient to harvest her organs to save other patients, it may be pertinent to include what we call the "self-defence clause". This clause would stipulate that exceptions such as the just war example are exceptions if and only if it is established that (1) the individuals involved are defending against human-made harm and (2) the facts of the matter (as it pertains to the reality of the potential human-made harm) are true.

---

[11] We take false self-interestedness as activities that seek (but ultimately fail) to improve one's well-being by undermining the well-being of others or by ignoring the interests of the collective. It describes what Innocent Asouzu (2004) calls the negative side of the ambivalence of human interests.

New terse statement:

> *An action is morally acceptable insofar as it augments one's vitality, and an action is morally wrong insofar as it diminishes one's vitality (or the vitality of others), except in cases where self-defence is necessary.*

There is also the question of altruistic acts, where one diminishes their vitality, even to the point of a total diminishing of their vitality, for the sake of increasing the vitality of others. This circumstance appears to be outside the purview of the vitalist principle. Metz makes this point clear when he argues that ' … a prescription to maximise one's own liveliness faces the problem of not sufficiently permitting, let alone requiring, one to give up one's life for others, since one's life would thereby end. This appears to be true even if those at risk were one's children and one could be assured of saving their lives (only) by ending one's own' (Metz, 2022, p. 82). One could, of course, arm-twist the vitalist view into accommodating such scenarios. Still, such a move would be unattractive since it would require the vitalist view to acquire a new identity that does not match its original identity. Perhaps one must bite the bullet and accept that altruism is not a part of the vitalist ethical narrative and that, instead, one ought to spend time deciphering whether this absence of altruism is a limitation or not. However, we believe that the self-defence clause aptly captures some forms of altruism. Consider the following example:

> A man, Steve Biko, who could have lived a less torturous life, decides to give up that possible life of relative ease to resist the oppression of a large group of people and become a freedom fighter. Let us suppose that prior to becoming a freedom fighter, it is quite clear that torture, imprisonment, illness, loneliness and the possibility of death are assured for anyone who would become a freedom fighter and that Steve knows this to be true. Nevertheless, he opts to become a freedom fighter, and he is tortured, imprisoned in solitary confinement, and then killed.

If our concerns about the vitality view are correct, then it must be true that Steve acted in an immoral way by clearly choosing to follow the path that led to a very visceral extinguishing of his vital force. But this is not the case by virtue of the self-defence clause. First, Steve shares a relationship with those who are being oppressed. This relationship can be direct (the sort that relates to things like being part of a family, community or country) or indirect (a sort of relationship that relies on the interconnected nature of things in the world, often intuited in African metaphysics). By showing that such a relationship exists between Steve and those who are oppressed, it becomes clear that harm to those oppressed people affects Steve negatively and harms him since Steve shares some ties with that oppressed group. Thus, since some individuals have proposed to consistently harm a certain group (which, in turn, harms Steve by virtue of his relationship, whether indirect or direct, with the oppressed group), Steve has the moral right[12] to defend himself and/or the oppressed group from harm, even if that would mean the loss of his (Steve's) life. In striving to defend his community, his vitality is augmented, as he is actively striving for the well-being of others. It is much the same way that a mother might put herself at risk of death to save her child(ren) from some morbid condition/encounter that threatens to harm them. Couched in this way, the self-defence clause does allow the vitalist theory to capture some altruistic acts.

However, a critic may be unsatisfied with our reply and claim that the present argument offered is too weak. They might further claim that the argument does not precisely show how the total diminution of vitality (the embodiment of morality, according to what we have proposed) is a moral act. To respond to this critique, we offer a last-ditch argument. This argument suggests that within the vitalist view, sacrificing one's vitality for the sake of other beings (in which case one willingly shares her vitality with others) is not morally bad (and is a duty in certain instances). The eldest in a community is, according to Tempels, supposed to '"reinforce" the life of his people and of all inferior forces, animal, vegetable and inorganic, that exist, grow, or live on the foundation which he provides for the welfare of his people.' (Tempels, 1959, p. 42). If Tempels is right, then it is true that any action that reinforces the life force of others, even by virtue of one's vitality (like the elder or chief that reinforces the vitality of his community by virtue of his own vitality), is not a morally bad one insofar as one's altruistic act, reinforces the life force of others. Now, perhaps some neat examples or thought experiments may undermine this argument, which is fair, but what we have done so far is show that the vitalist view can attempt a response to the issue of altruism.

Next, we deal with an interesting problem. And this problem has to do with questions related to the following: since vitality embodies morality (as we suggested in one instance), are all diminutions of vitality immoral? Suppose Mr P came to an accident and is paralysed. He has surely lost some vitality, but would that mean he did something immoral? To answer this question, we must first remember that for human beings, our vitality is of a special kind since it is supposedly imbued with consciousness (where rationality eventually springs from the type of consciousness we possess, which other lower beings presumably do not share), which is the one thing that makes the vitality we possess most Godlike. And so, one argument that could be advanced in response is that any loss of vitality that does not spring from this distinguishing Godlike

---

[12] We are currently unsure whether it is also a duty.

property is less a matter of morality. Mr P, in our example, would have experienced harm but not an immoral one since the cause of his reduced vitality is an unconscious cause (a less Godlike cause).

To further buttress this point, we appeal to *intention* and *action* as important categories that help us home in on acts that touch on this God-property of vitality. Intention is understood here to mean conceiving of an action and establishing the will to carry out that action. Action, on the other hand, refers to the expression of any form of ontological capacities (in this context, the type that has to do with the human body) – whether movement, speaking, and so on. Now, where both intention and action are present, one can ask questions about whether or not an individual is *doing* something morally right or wrong. Indeed, as Tempels (1959) notes, within the vitalist view, intentionally committed acts of evil are especially bad. So, when an individual extinguishes the life force of another person via murder, that individual is doing something morally wrong since the expression of intention touches on that Godlike feature in the vital force. Where action alone is present (that is, where an individual acts unintentionally), then questions about morality are pushed to the background, and the focus shifts from the actor to the moral patient. Thus, it is not that the actor/moral agent has done something morally right or wrong; it is that the moral patient has experienced something good or bad. So, when an individual 'A' accidentally trips on a banana skin and lands on a lever that causes another item to injure another individual, 'B', it is not the case that 'A' did something morally wrong even though B experienced some loss of vitality, but it is the case that B experienced something bad (the diminution of B's vitality through injury). Where there is only intention, the situation becomes tricky. If an individual always spends time intending to extinguish the vitality of others, is that individual doing something morally wrong? To answer this question, one observation by Tempels comes to mind. According to him:

> All enmity, hatred, envy, jealousy, evil speaking, even false praise or lying eulogy, are severely condemned by the Bantu. To anyone who allows his envy or hatred to rise, the reproach is addressed 'Do you want to kill me? Have you bufwisi or buloji in your heart?' (Tempels, 1959, p. 82)

Things like hatred, envy, and jealousy are not always performative and can be grouped under what we call bad intentions. Indeed, in an earlier statement, Tempels notes that, for the Bantu, *Buloji*, or diabolical evil, is something that emanates from within and then contaminates relationships. To have *Buloji* is to possess something bad and repulsive. Evil or bad intentions, according to the vitalist view, are a type of perversion or corruption of the Godlike feature of consciousness. Thus, from the foregoing, one need not express one's bad intention in some performative way; merely harbouring evil intentions is enough to corrupt one's vitality, and this allows us to claim that in one version of the vitalist view, harbouring bad intentions is morally bad since it undermines one's vitality.

5 Vitality and Dignity

One question that has ramifications in law, ethics, social and political relations, and so on, is the question of human dignity. This is a question about what, if anything, makes the human being special and worthy of a high level of moral regard. According to Molefe:

> The concept of dignity refers to the intrinsic worth associated with some entity in virtue of possessing certain ontological features .... Dignity marks something, in virtue of possessing certain ontological features or capacities, as having a superlative rank ... (Molefe, 2020, p. 1)

Finding such a feature is not as easy and uncomplicated as one may imagine. Take the Kantian approach, for instance. The usual move for adherents of this approach is to locate human dignity in something like our capacity to set goals or our capacity for morality (Pele, 2016). However, such a view fails to show how young infants or individuals born with severe cognitive abilities might possess dignity. Of course, one can add potentiality into the mix, but such a move does not take care of our intuition that in cases where a trade-off is necessary between an adult human being and, say, a human zygote or embryo in a petri dish, many would believe that there are good reasons to consider the adult human being first. Beyond this, the fact remains that potentiality is not actuality, and to equate the two would be to take an uncomfortable inductive leap – it is, for instance, true that we do have the potential to be the president of our countries but we would most likely contend with armed law enforcement if we marched to the seat of power and expected to make decisions as 'potential' presidents. In African thought, one may attempt to locate dignity in the capacity for communion (see Metz, 2012). Again, the same problems identified above might arise. How does one account for the dignity of infants who are only objects of communion? One move would be to relax the requirements to involve being an object of communion. But then, would pets, for instance, possess dignity?

All these questions are important because if we want to establish a grounding for human dignity – one that has real-world consequences for how we treat other persons – such a grounding must be strong and resistant to a significant amount of criticism. A conception of dignity that is based on the idea of vitality may present itself as a viable candidate. It is important to note here that we do not claim that a vitalist conception of dignity is the most viable theory of dignity.

Rather, since this is an Element on vitality, it is pertinent that we present, examine, and discuss plausible conceptions of human dignity that are based on the notion of vital force.

Traditional Vitalist Conception of Dignity

When examining the traditional notions of vitality, as found in the literature, one immediately sees how the vital force can stand as that special feature that distinguishes the human being from other physical things in the world. To understand what we mean, we must remind ourselves of the hierarchy of being in traditional African religions and philosophies. In this hierarchy, human beings stand on top of the ladder as far as physical things are concerned, so they are thought of as having more value than plants, animals, or inanimate things. Even so, human beings remain at the bottom of the ladder when it comes to quasi-physical and/or non-physical things with the Godlike property of consciousness, and so ancestors and spirits have more value/power than human beings, with God or the Supreme Being at the top of that hierarchy. Now, within the context of the traditional vitality view, what sustains this hierarchy is the manner in which the vital force is distributed to all realities. In Section 1, we have shown that God, or the Supreme Being, sits at the top of this hierarchy because God is believed to be the source and the embodiment of this vital force. Inanimate things, like rocks and metals, sit at the bottom of the hierarchy because they possess the lowest amounts of vital energy compared to plants and animals. Human beings, on the other hand, tower, in value, over other physical entities because they not only possess more vital energy, but their vitality is imbued with the Godlike properties of consciousness, rationality, and creative power (more so than any other physical entity in the world), which are all Godlike properties. For the traditional vitalist, we have finally struck at what makes humans particularly special: the vital force (imbued with the Godlike feature of consciousness, rationality, and creative power). In this way, traditional vitalists would presume that the proper grounding for human dignity would be the vital force, such that if one had vitality, the type that humans are imbued with, then such an individual would have dignity.

Now, there are a few ways in which the traditional vitalist view of dignity can be cashed out. First, the possession of the ontological feature – vital force (the type imbued with the above-mentioned Godlike properties) – is enough to ground dignity. In other words, insofar as a human being is the type of being it is – an entity that possesses a high quantity (more vitality than animals, plants, and inanimate things) and quality (intellectually sophisticated and conscious) of vital force – the human being possesses dignity. Some questions would suffice at this point. Suppose an individual was at the point of death, her vital force greatly diminished, would she have as much dignity as, say, a vibrant Chimpanzee or Orangutan that is alive and well? If the quantity and quality of vitality are what grant dignity, what happens when an individual's dignity is greatly diminished, and/or what happens if an individual is severely disabled, cognitively speaking? These are difficult questions, and friends of the traditional vitalist view might respond in several ways.

First, they might say that the dignity criteria should now focus squarely on the Godlike feature of consciousness, intelligence, and/or creative power rather than the quantity of vitality that an individual or thing has. Thus, insofar as an individual is conscious, that individual has dignity. But this move does not tell us whether or how individuals in a vegetative state or experiencing some sort of severe cognitive disability would possess dignity. In fact, left this way, the current view would suggest that individuals in a coma lack dignity, but this is counter-intuitive. With this in mind, friends of the traditional vitalist view might respond by saying that insofar as a being is alive and possesses (even if) a spectre of vitality that is imbued with the Godlike features mentioned in this section, such a being has dignity. And so, an individual in a coma or with a severe disability still possesses a spectre of this Godlike vitality, and so does possess dignity.

Advocates of the traditional vitalist view might also answer the question in another way. They might proceed to appeal to the membership of the human species as a co-grounding for dignity. Accordingly, they might say that humans are precisely the only sort of beings that could be the appropriate receptacles for the type of vitality that contains the quality and quantity of Godlike vitality that human beings possess. In the same way that Chimpanzees or Orangutans might never usurp human beings in the hierarchy of beings because they are not the sort of receptacles that could house the type of vitality that humans possess, humans can never be the supreme being since their very nature can never be a receptacle for the quantity and quality of vitality that the Supreme Being possesses. And so, by virtue of being the type of receptacle that human beings are, any member of the human species, insofar as they are alive, possesses a base dignity that surpasses that of any other animal or plant. This base grounding suggests that all humans are born with dignity since they are the sort of beings that can possess the human kind of vitality.

However, despite this base grounding for dignity, there is also the intuition that suggests that there is a gradation of dignity among various human beings. This thinking is informed by the idea that one's actions, relationship with God and other human beings, good health, as well as the type of malevolence one gives out or receives from other beings, and so on, can all affect the levels of vitality in one's life. If this is true, then one must admit that human beings possess vitality in varying degrees, and the more vital force an individual possesses, the more dignified (worthy of respect, esteem, and admiration) the individual. Thus, individuals who have made great contributions to promoting vitality in themselves and others would have a higher degree of dignity than those who do not. Take the life of Nelson Mandela. Having developed certain virtues in himself and having fought to ensure that an oppressive state of affairs does not undermine the vitality of South Africans, he presumably possesses more vitality than a fair number of people who lead average lives. By this thinking, Nelson Mandela would possess a greater degree of dignity than the average person. This might perhaps account for the special treatment Mr Mandela received towards the later stages of his life compared to, say, any of the writers of this Element. In the same vein, individuals like Leopold II of Belgium, who was responsible for reducing and snuffing out the vitality of tens of millions of Africans, would have very low levels of vitality, and so a very low level of dignity, although he would still be thought of as having more dignity than, say, a goat.

From the foregoing, it becomes clear that one could act in ways that deny them a higher degree of vitality/dignity and that one can act in ways that augment their dignity/vitality. But here, we make an important distinction. While all human beings have dignity, some individuals might live a more dignified life than others. While dignity would imply possessing inherent worth (the type of vitality that human beings possess), a dignified life implies a life that commands honour, recognition, and respect (and expressing that worth in positive ways). So, while one might lead a less dignified life, this would not necessarily imply that the individual has no inherent worth or dignity.

The Naturalistic Vitalist View of Dignity

In the preceding, we have seen that the traditional vitalist conception of dignity depends on a supernaturalistic understanding of the view. However, Metz claims that the vitalist view can also be explained in naturalistic terms. This move relies heavily on how other African philosophers have spoken about vitality as an expression of features that are decidedly natural. According to Metz, some African scholars take it to be true that exhibiting 'a superlative degree of health, strength, growth, reproduction, creativity, vibrancy, activity, self-motion, courage and confidence ... ' is exhibiting vitality, while 'a lack of life force ... [is] constituted by the presence of disease, weakness, decay, barrenness, destruction, lethargy, passivity, submission, insecurity and depression' (Metz, 2012, p. 25). He goes on to list some scholars, like Dzobo (1992), Peter Kasenene (1994), Laurent Magesa (1997), and Nhlanhla Mkhize (2008), as representatives of this viewpoint.

Now, all the features that have been listed in this section do not require supernaturalism to make sense. If this is true, and if it is true that these features or properties express vitality, then it is plausible to construct a naturalist conception of vitality from African thought, which would then ground a secular vitalist conception of dignity. And this is precisely what Metz does. To emphasise this naturalistic orientation, Metz calls his naturalistic view of vitality 'liveliness' or 'creative power' (used interchangeably). Metz appeals to (and prefers) this naturalistic view to the supernaturalistic view for three related reasons:

> First, the naturalist or physical construals of the vitality conception are no less compelling than the supernaturalist or spiritual ones; indeed, the former might be more compelling than the latter in that they account better for, e.g. the human right to life and correlative degradingness of murder. Second, most of us are much more confident that we have a dignity than that we have any spiritual nature, meaning that we cannot coherently ground a conception of dignity on spiritual notions. Third, even if we do have a spiritual nature, or are confident that we do, it would be inappropriate to ground political decision making on such a contested conception of the good, and I seek a theory of dignity that should ground legislative choice and judicial interpretation. (Metz, 2012, p. 25).

Indeed, at the heart of Metz's preference for a naturalistic view of vitality is the idea that grounding vitality on the easily debatable idea of a *spiritual* essence is problematic. If we cannot, for certain, establish the existence of this spiritual energy beyond speculation, then there is little reason to take the view seriously. And if one intends to ground something with as much moral relevance as human dignity on ideas that are debatable, then one is grounding human dignity on a shaky foundation. The naturalistic view avoids this problem since features such as 'health, strength, growth, reproduction, creativity, vibrancy, activity, self-motion, courage and confidence ... ' (Metz, 2012, p. 25) are natural features of the human being that do not require much debate to establish. Thus, grounding the vitalist conception of dignity on this naturalistic conception of vitality is building it on a much firmer ground that is less bound to speculation; at least, Metz would agree.

On this naturalistic notion of vitality, human dignity – what makes us special in relation to animals, plants, and inanimate things, and what demands our special treatment – is 'roughly that we have a much greater liveliness or creative power than they' (Metz, 2012, p. 25). Metz goes on to note that, based on the liveliness view of dignity, human beings ought to be treated with respect insofar as they possess the capacity for creative power or liveliness (note that dignity inheres in the capacity for liveliness and not in the display/pursuit of more liveliness). Conversely, degrading or violating one's dignity is to severely degrade one's capacity for liveliness. Thus, when human beings act in ways (or set up policies) that unduly undermine another individual's health, strength, growth, reproduction, creativity, vibrancy, activity, self-motion, courage, and confidence, they violate that individual's dignity.

6 Vitality and Meaning in Life

The question of whether or not life has meaning or whether or not moments in life can be considered meaningful is, for us, a philosophical question above all philosophical questions. While this question had been largely ignored by African philosophers in the past, apart from Munyaradzi Mawere's (2010) article on the topic and hints by the likes of Kwasi Wiredu and Monday Igbafen, the discussion on life's meaning from an African perspective only began to receive new life in 2019–2020, following a Workshop on 'African Conceptions of the Meaning of Life', held at the University of Johannesburg and the publication of a Special Issue by the *South African Journal of Philosophy* (2020). In these works, the vitalist view has entrenched itself as a strong contender for a viable conception of meaning in life, with scholars like Attoe (2020, 2023), Metz (2020), Mlungwana (2020), and Agada (2020a) all proposing plausible conceptions of meaning in life based on the vitalist view.

In what follows, we intend to provide the reader with a brief account of the vitalist conception of meaning in its 'traditional' form and also provide an account of those conceptions of meaning that have evolved out of this traditional view.

The Traditional Religious View

To unpack this view, we must go back to the traditional conception of vitality discussed in the previous section. As we have seen, the vital force is the animating principle, a sort of spiritual force that drives the activity of everything that exists in the world – although in varying degrees. According to Dukor (quoted from Wilfred Lajul), 'Africans believe that behind every human being or object there is a vital power or soul ... Africans personify nature because they believe that there is a spiritual force residing in every object of nature' (Lajul, 2017, p. 28). While vital force permeates all of reality in varying degrees, humans, at the very least, and unlike other animals, plants, or inanimate things, are able to pursue meaning because the vital force we possess is of a special kind – it contains the Godlike features of consciousness, rationality, and/or creative power. As Deogratia Bikopo and Louis-Jacques van Bogaert note:

> All beings are endowed with varying levels of energy. The highest levels characterise the Supreme Being (God), the 'Strong One'; the *muntu* (person, intelligent being), participates in God's force, and so do the non-human animals but to a lesser degree ... Life has its origin in *Ashé*, power, the creative source of all that is. This power gives vitality to life and dynamism to being. *Ashé* is the creative word, the logos; it is: 'A rational and spiritual principle that confers identity and destiny to humans.' ... What subsists after death is the 'self' that was hidden behind the body during life. The process of dying is not static; it goes through progressive stages of energy loss. To be dead means to have a diminished life because of a reduced level of energy. When the level of energy falls to zero, one is completely dead. (Bikopo & van Bogaert, 2010, pp. 44–45)

From the above, we are introduced to a crucial aspect of the view, which is the idea that levels of vitality are not static but are dynamic, and it is this fluctuation in levels of vitality that ultimately determines the quality of an individual's life. Even more crucial is the idea that this vitality can be augmented and diminished by human action and by the actions of other rational beings other than the human being (God, ancestors and the like). According to Tempels:

> Man (living or deceased) can directly reinforce or diminish the being of another man. Such vital influence is possible from man to man: it is indeed necessarily effective as between the progenitor, a superior vital force, – and his progeny – an inferior force ... A rational being (spirit, manes, or living) can act indirectly upon another rational being by communicating his vital influence to an inferior force (animal, vegetable, or mineral) through the intermediacy of which it influences the rational being. This influence will also have the character of a necessarily effective action, save only when the object is inherently the stronger force, or is reinforced by the influence of some third party, or preserves himself by recourse to inferior forces exceeding those which his enemy is employing. (Tempels, 1959, pp. 45–46)

He goes further to state that:

> According to Bantu thought, it is, then, logical that the 'muntu' should be able to grow ontologically, become greater, stronger; and equally that he should be able, as 'muntu', to diminish, lose his vital force and come to an end in the complete annihilation of his very essence, the paralysis of his vital force, which takes from him the power to be an active force, a vital cause. (Tempels, 1959, p. 66)

From the preceding, it is clear that the quality of one's life largely depends on the levels of vitality in one's life. Furthermore, individuals can and should take active steps to augment their vitality and take further steps to avoid diminishing it. To increase one's vitality, a relationship with God is important since God is perceived as the ultimate source of vitality in this traditional view. Thus, worshipping God, performing certain rituals, and praying are essential ingredients for augmenting one's vitality and, by extension, the quality of one's life.

Furthermore, in our relationship with other persons in the world, values such as fairness and justice, compassion and mutual sharing are the sorts of things that augment not only one's vital force but the vitality of the recipient of such other-regarding actions. In one's relationship with oneself, actions that seek to improve one's happiness, ensure one's happiness and prevent one from more powerful malevolent individuals or forces are also essential in sustaining one's vitality. In terms of the diminution of one's vitality, one must avoid negative experiences such as suffering, depression, injustice, illness, and so on. These experiences may be caused by negligent behaviour towards ourselves, negative relationships with other people, and a lack of protection against undue malevolence.

From the above, we begin to get a sense of what meaning in life would entail within the context of traditional ideas about vitalism. According to this view, a meaningful life would involve a high degree of vitality sustained over the course of one's life. Meaningful acts, or moments of meaning, would include those actions/moments that serve to increase or augment one's vitality. These would consist of engaging in positive other-regarding activities (showing love and compassion, sharing with others, pursuing the common good, etc.) and being a recipient/beneficiary of such activities, engaging in certain rituals, worshipping God, and so on. A meaningless life, on the other hand, would be a life of sustained low levels of vitality – usually a life characterised by suffering, illness, depression, and alienation. Meaningless acts, or moments of meaninglessness, would involve the experience of vitality-draining activities or state of affairs such as being a victim of malevolence, being malevolent towards others, experiencing moments of failure and suffering, being a victim of a debilitating illness, and so on (Agada, 2020a; Attoe, 2020; Mlungwana, 2020).

This sentiment is also shared by Metz (2020, p. 119), who, in his description of the vitalist account, similarly notes that the promotion of vitality (whether one thinks of it in natural or supernatural terms) equates to the promotion of meaning in one's life. Even more interesting is his description of the process of promoting vitality as (what one may call) an internal and external process. The internal process involves 'developing vitality in oneself, traditionally to the point where one's vital force is so strong as to become an ancestor'. This would normally involve the cultivation of certain virtues that would allow the individual to pursue those activities that foster vitality. As for the external process,

Metz notes that promoting vitality (and, therefore, meaning) can also mean helping others foster their own vitality/meaning. In this instance, Metz describes this route to meaning as purposing to produce in others 'properties such as health, growth, reproduction, creativity, vibrancy, activity, self-motion, courage, and confidence'. Beyond actively fostering such properties in others, meaningfulness also involves *preventing* or *reducing* properties/circumstances in others that would reduce their vitality. He makes this point when he states that 'one's purpose is also to reduce in others properties that include disease, decay, barrenness, destruction, lethargy, passivity, submission, insecurity, and depression. I suppose here that the most promising account of meaning includes both oneself and others as relevant sites of liveliness' (Metz, 2020, p. 119).

Another African philosopher, Agada, categorises vitalist accounts of meaning similarly. For Agada (2020a), the vital force has ontological and psychological dimensions. While the ontological dimension refers to the all-pervading force or cosmic energy itself (which he takes to be neither wholly material nor immaterial), the psychological dimension refers to 'affects such as joy and sadness' that generally capture the subjective/psychological demeanour of the individual in relation to the zest for life or the lack of it (Agada, 2020a, p. 103). Agada (2020a, p. 103) maintains that this psychological dimension of joy and sadness only operates in the 'sphere of sentient and thinking being'.[13] Like Metz, and in line with the traditional view, Agada (2020a, p. 103) also agrees that 'a meaningful life will be one that maximises vital force in all aspects of a person's life.' The maximising of vitality, for Agada, would not only involve the maximisation of vitality at the ontological level (for instance, through prayer, and ritual), it would also involve pursuing and maximising optimistic states of mind (as per the psychological dimension) rather than negative states of mind – in other words, one must maximise joy and minimise sadness.

According to him:

> Positive states of mind and affects like optimism, hopefulness and joy are to be maximised, while negative states of mind and affects like pessimism, nihilism, fearfulness and sadness are to be minimised. Knowledge must be pursued and ignorance rejected. The inability or failure to maximise vital force leads to a greatly diminished existence and an increasingly meaningless life. (Agada, 2020a, p. 103)

---

[13] While this view obviously serves to locate meaning in the domain of human beings and other thinking beings (ancestors, God, etc.), one wonders whether the inclusion of sentient beings implies that non-human sentient beings, such as certain animals, can have/pursue meaningful lives, or lead meaningless lives. This would have implications for how humans relate to such beings, and their duties to such beings. Agada does not pursue this line of thought in this essay but we believe it is worth drawing our attention to this point.

While meaning might involve subjective pursuits and benefits in the traditional vitalist account, the psychological dimension that Agada refers to makes it imperative that meaningful pursuit is a collective effort. We say this because negative states of mind (which must be avoided) often express themselves as a response to events in one's environment and a reaction to our relationships with other things in the world. To create meaning, even with respect to the psychological dimension, one must (as Metz notes) seek the well-being of one's self and others, as this fosters the type of environment/experiences that would allow for the kind of joy that Agada envisions.

Mood, Vitality, Consolation, and Meaning in Life

One of the more profound philosophical systems in African thought is the theory of consolationism, propounded by Nigerian Philosopher Ada Agada. Central to consolationism is the idea of mood, which presents itself as a primordial, all-pervading, and fundamental principle that is present in all things and, supposedly, instantiates the mystery of mind and the physicality of material things. Indeed, Agada describes the strength of the concept of mood as lying in its ability to navigate between the extremes of reductive/eliminative materialism (where consciousness is reduced to neural function) and panpsychism (which considers mind or consciousness the only fundamental reality).

Immediately, one begins to notice the similarities between mood and vital force, and it comes as little surprise that Agada proceeds to ground his idea of mood on the idea of vital force since both concepts purport to describe an all-pervading and primordial entity that animates all reality in varying degrees. Grounding mood in vitality and subsequently reconceptualising vitality in terms of mood, Agada makes the claim of revolutionising, quite radically, the idea of vital force into the idea of mood.

But what is mood? Agada provides us with the following definition:

> ... *[M]ood* is: [A] proto-mind and primordial intelligence ubiquitous in the universe and characterized by yearning ... the most fundamental reality; it is the essence of things, implicating reasons, feelings, dispositions, orientations, and affects, both conscious and unconscious. As proto-mind, *mood* is originary intelligence and feeling, containing within itself the conditions of growth and development, from the level of rudimentary consciousness to the most advanced level possible. It motivates the activities of all things as their essence. Everything in the universe is a development of *mood*, both the animate and the inanimate. Rationality unfolds out of *mood* and reaches various degrees of development in entities. It is a proto-mind in the sense of being mind-like and primordial. (Agada, 2019, p. 4)

Agada's conceptualisation of mood (and, in turn, his reconceptualisation of vitality) tells us a few things. First, it is a primordial reality that, in its primordiality, is the fundamental thing that instantiates both mind/consciousness and body. In this way, reality, as we know it, is not only animated by mood/vitality but is fundamentally constituted by mood. In our interpretation of this view, mood must exist as the first cause if we are to believe that all that exists is instantiated by mood. But mood, in its primordial form, is not pure and sophisticated consciousness, and so, for the consolationist, mood must predate God,[14] if God is a being (since mood instantiates being) and a conscious being (since consciousness is not a direct feature of mood in its natural form as protomind). In a way, Agada's reconceptualisation of vitality as mood aligns with the traditional view and, at the same time, radically departs from it. In terms of the former, God is conceived as the most sophisticated instantiation of mood in much the same way that God is viewed as the embodiment of vitality. The radical departure would then be the implication that God cannot be the source of mood/vitality since God is merely an instance, even though a radical instantiation, of mood – which goes against the traditional view of vitality that projects God as the *source* of vital force.

The second point in Agada's definition of mood is the idea that mood *motivates* reality. The word motivation here is key as we discuss life's meaning in terms of mood. We shall explain presently. One can glean from Agada (2022) that what motivates reality is what he refers to as 'yearning'. Yearning, briefly, can be described as the pursuit of perfection. This yearning allows different forms of reality to continue evolving in various ways in this search for perfection. Agada further states, with some conviction, that yearning is 'empirically evidenced' by the 'endless quest by animals, and vegetable life for food, mate, and progress, and in the seemingly inanimate sphere by the constant interaction of subatomic particles that suggests an underlying method to the chaotic constant' (Agada, 2022, p. 75). Yearning, being a necessary feature of mood, also animates mood. For instance, it is this yearning that activates the instantiation of things in the world, and it is this yearning that also allows for the animation of the same instantiated things via the move towards perfection.

What, then, would meaning in life entail within the framework of mood? Agada provides a robust enough answer for us to work with. First, we observe that from yearning (the motivating essence that animates mood and being), reality, as a whole, and the human being in particular, is oriented towards

---

[14] It is unclear how any being, instantiated by mood, is worthy of the moniker 'God'. Although Agada mentions power and glory as the very features that make God God, Attoe is unconvinced.

perfection. From this orientation, Agada intuits that the purpose of existence is the pursuit of perfection. This perfection, as Agada (2022, p. 76) defines it, is the 'fullest actual terminus of progress that makes everything whole and good, eliminating pain [evil] and death and establishing why humans and the universe exist.' Perfection, in other words, is a state of affairs that captures absolute joy and zero sadness (using Agada's terms) and forms the fundamental desire of all beings, even down to the primordial mood itself. In human beings, the pursuit of joy is expressed in precisely those activities that are thought to enliven the individual or increase their vitality (as seen in the traditional view). Of course, this involves the normative requirement to be other-regarding as a way of building vitality and the encouragement to tap into vitality through social rituals and the worship of God. For a more contemporary audience, the search for joy or vitality often involves the pursuit of money, sex, technology, social media, and so on, as sources of vitality and joy. And so, in Agada's reconceptualisation of vitality, in terms of mood, meaning in life lies in the active pursuit of perfection (not just the yearning for perfection, which is the natural state of all beings). But as one would have guessed, these sorts of pursuits, at best, provide an occasion for momentary joy and not the type envisioned in the state of perfection.

In many cases, the prospect of joy is ambivalent, in the sense that what is pursued as joy often bequeaths sadness to the unfortunate yearning being. Furthermore, perfection and joy require the transformation of conscious beings from imperfect entities to eternal and morally perfect beings, living in a world of things whose interaction with each other must be absolutely beneficial to all that exists, since the absolute joy of being encapsulates perfection. This, coupled with the inevitable sadness and seeming finality of death (for every instantiation of human consciousness), closes the lid on the idea that perfection could ever be attained, no matter how grandiose or noble our pursuit of that perfection.

At the very least, perfection is an impossible task for human beings, so the pursuit of perfection, occasioned by the yearning for perfection (which is an essential feature of human beings), is futile. This, for Agada, is the sad tragedy of existence – that we are locked in the pursuit of an unattainable ideal. It is this tragedy, and the realisation of this tragedy by the sophisticated consciousness of the human being, that allows Agada to bestow upon human beings the label of *Homo Melancholicus* (i.e., melancholy being).

This tragedy extends to all realities, as all living and non-living realities cannot attain perfection. But this should come as no surprise. Perfection is not part and parcel of being, even at the most fundamental level of mood, and this absence, even in potentiality, exposes the folly of this primordial yearning for perfection.

As tragic beings living in a tragic world, the possibility of attaining ultimate meaning is non-existent, as Agada rightly intuits. However, in the yearning and pursuit of freedom, we come to realise that we do, indeed, encounter momentary and/or significant moments of joy. It is in these moments of joy that we encounter short-lived moments of meaningfulness. Thus, the totalising tragedy of existing in futility (by yearning for and pursuing a purpose that is inherently unachievable) is not so total as to wholly transform moments of joy in themselves into something negative. So, in that moment of joy, the individual attains some level of meaning in life, regardless of the overall futility of existence.

Now, one might respond by questioning the utility of momentary joy or meaning in life, even if significant, when the inevitable end demands that life be recognised as meaningless. How would one reconcile these two contrary positions and still retain the usefulness of momentary joy?

Agada has this to say:

> Striving never reaches its ultimate goal, but in the process of striving certain goals are realized to meet the yearnings of the striving entity even as achievements ultimately count for nothing. This insight informs the labelling of my system *consolation* philosophy. (Agada, 2020b, p. 112)

Agada's position reveals a few things when considered closely. First is the idea that momentary joy or momentary meaning in life can serve as a *consolation* for the ultimate meaninglessness and tragedy of existence. This consolation, in this instance, is not hope for meaning, although it could serve as a source of false hope for many who refuse to acknowledge the inevitable (whether due to denial or due to ignorance). Instead, it serves as a sort of palliative that temporarily relieves the pain that comes with realising our tragic existence.

The Liveliness Conception of Meaning in Life

One can point to Metz as the first to systematically articulate a coherent theory of meaning that is naturalistic (yet based mainly on the idea of vitality), which he refers to as "liveliness", following the earlier foundations laid by Dzobo (1992). Other traces of the view can be found in Metz's earlier work on a vitalist conception of dignity. To understand the liveliness view on meaning in life, it is pertinent that we begin the discussion by drawing out some of these preliminary viewpoints, which would then set the stage for our description of the liveliness view.

In describing vitality, Dzobo makes the following remarks:

> Since the essence of the ideal life is regarded as power and creativity, growth, creative work and increase have become essential values. Powerlessness or loss of Vitality, unproductive living and growthlessness become ultimate

> evils in our indigenous culture. For many Africans one of man's chief ends as an individual and as a member of an extended family is to multiply and increase, because he is the repository of the life force, and the right use of it is his responsibility. The loss of vitality, i.e., impotence, is therefore the worst tragedy that can happen to a man; to a woman it is infertility. (Dzobo, 1992, p. 227)

From Dzobo's remark, one immediately notices a shift from describing vitality only in religious/supernaturalistic terms to describing vitality in terms that are relatable to beings living in the physical (i.e., in naturalistic terms). Thus, rather than merely speaking about spiritual or cosmic energy, Dzobo (1992, p. 227) describes vitality in terms of values such as 'power and creativity, growth, creative work and increase [fertility].' Now, these terms/values can be thought of as excisable from talk of supernaturalism. Creativity or creative power might speak to an individual's capacity to create new things or bring new ideas or objects into existence (think of the many ideas and inventions humans have managed so far). Growth and increase can be cashed out in terms of general well-being and success, whether in terms of one's health, activities, character, productivity, and/or procreation. Notice that in these descriptions, there is no talk of a supernatural entity (such as God) who is the source of vitality; neither is there any talk of spiritual energy (even though the values described above point to vitality).

So, two possibilities are plausible in Dzobo's conception of vitality. First, vital energy, as a spiritual force, can manifest itself in decidedly natural values/activities. Pursuing these activities increases our vital force (the spiritual/immaterial energy). Already, Ada Agada has previously noted that the interaction between vital force and the material body, and, one can add, the possibility of natural activities affecting one's level of vitality, combine to suggest that, at the very least, the vital force is not wholly immaterial/spiritual. Second, it is possible to disregard talk of supernaturality and refer to vitality only in terms of these natural values/pursuits. And so, it is possible to *naturalise* the concept of vital force, if Dzobo is to be taken seriously. This is precisely what Metz (2012) does as he approaches the idea of vitality from a naturalistic standpoint (as we have already stated in the section on liveliness and dignity).

Following this, Metz develops liveliness as a theory of meaning in life when he states:

> I suppose here that the most promising [vitalist] account of meaning includes both oneself and others as relevant sites of liveliness. Consider, then, the *vitalist theory of meaning*: A human person's life is more meaningful, the more that she promotes liveliness in herself and others. (Metz, 2020, pp. 119–120)

From this view, insofar as one is able to promote liveliness in oneself and in others, that individual is living a meaningful life. The promotion of liveliness (and, therefore, meaning) would involve engaging in those activities that engender good health, growth, reproduction/procreation, creativity, and so on, in one's life and the life of others. Thus, when one acts benevolently to others or cares for them in ways that allow them to overcome an illness and live a healthy life or in ways that promote their general well-being, one is acting meaningfully. Also, when one creates something new or novel, such an individual is promoting liveliness and, by extension, meaning in life.

Conversely, an extreme solitary life (Metz uses the example of being hooked up to an experience machine or being in solitary confinement), is a meaningless life mainly because of the inability to adequately promote liveliness in one's self and in others (since opportunities for growth, use of creative power, and so on, are unavailable to such an individual). Also, when one engages in acts that are severely immoral (Metz uses the example of rape and slavery), one is not only failing at promoting vitality (and living a meaningful life) but also taking away the vitality of others (the victims of such actions).

Part III Some Critiques of the Vital Force Theory

7 A Racial Foundation

For scholars like Asouzu (2007) and Matolino (Imafidon et al., 2019), there is a problem in the way in which the vitalist view was couched by Tempels [whose attempt to articulate an African philosophy was among the first attempts in what Chimakonam (2014) now calls systematic African philosophy]. Both scholars are scathing in their critique of Tempels' project as well as projects built on a similar methodological framework.

For Asouzu, the problem with Tempels' view (what he calls the 'Tempelsian damage') starts from the use of Aristotelian metaphysics (which he calls elitist and bifurcating) to examine Bantu metaphysics. Asouzu claims that Tempels used the idea of vitality as a smoke screen to entrench the view that Bantu metaphysics is a debased form of rationality and non-transcendental metaphysics (beyond superstitions and magic) when compared with Western metaphysics (Asouzu, 2007b). By claiming, as Tempels (1959, p. 34) does, that '[w]e [the West] can conceive the transcendental notion of "being" by separating it from its attribute, "Force", but the Bantu cannot. [And that] we hold a static conception of "being", they a dynamic', Tempels is (un)intentionally suggesting that Bantu ontology and metaphysicians lack the inherent ability/capacity for transcendental/abstract views. Indeed, Tempels further states: 'We do not claim, of course, that the Bantu are capable of formulating a philosophical treatise, complete with an adequate vocabulary. It is our job to proceed to such systematic development. It is we who will be able to tell them, in precise terms, what their inmost concept of being is. ' (Tempels, 1959, p. 23). One can then imagine that in the re-articulation of Bantu thought, distortions are inevitable from the eyes of an individual whose logic of comprehension is different.

It is, thus, strange, for Asouzu, that it is this vitalist ontology, with its colonial underpinnings and its many distortions, that is 'being paraded in many quarters today as the very essence of African ontology and experience of reality' (2007b, p. 75). Even more unfortunate, says Asouzu, is the difficulty in exorcising Tempels' ghost, as it pertains to the idea of vitality, since the view is ideologically attractive, as it projects an ontology that is sufficiently different from 'Western' metaphysics, as African philosophy searches for its unique identity.

Matolino, in his critique of Tempels' project, does not stray too far from Asouzu. Matolino is particularly scathing in his critique of Tempels' project. According to Matolino:

> If we look closely at both the intentions and contents of his book Bantu Philosophy, a signature reference of all the ills of ethnophilosophy, we find an intriguing combination of racism and colonial fawning. Tempels does not hide what his intentions are: they are to aid the success of the colonial mission. ... in order to succeed at the mission to civilize, the differences that exist between the black and white person must be laid bare. The purpose of exposing those differences is meant to demonstrate how the black person is inferior to the white person. Even when Tempels pulls the greatest historical trick of claiming equivalence between force and being, it is his mystification of force both in definition and illustration that proves that the black person is inferior to her white counterpart. Tempels does not begin his project to guarantee the equality of the races so that the black person can be freed so she can enjoy the political liberties that the white person has. On the contrary, the black person is in need of civilization and continued patronage of the white person which comes in the form of the mission to civilize. (Imafidon et al., 2019, p. 116)

The main claim here is that the foundation on which the idea of vitality was originally conceived was/is a distorted foundation – one where the ontological views of the Bantu are deliberately distorted to portray difference for the sake of the colonial project. These distortions are real and fundamental. Tempels, for instance, claims that force is equivalent to being, an ontological claim that is crucial to the vital force view. Yet, for Matolino, this claim is a trick – one that continues to be projected as an authentic African notion of being. This trick, for Matolino, does not have its roots in reality but primarily in the need to differentiate the Bantu from the West, to inferiorise the Bantu, and to establish the need for a colonial project. This last point is further exacerbated by other claims that Tempels himself made; for instance, in a revised hierarchy of being, Tempels appears to place Europeans on a higher pedestal than all Africans. Tempels claims:

> The technological skill of the White man impressed the Bantu. The White man seemed to be the master of great natural forces. It had, therefore, to be admitted that the White man was an elder, a superior human force, surpassing vital force of all Africans. (Tempels, 1959, p. 43)

If Asouzu and Matolino are both right in their critiques, then one would have to be suspicious of the whole vitalist project as one that is, at the very least, deeply flawed in many respects. Now, it is difficult to refute Asouzu's and Matolino's arguments, and, by extension, it is also difficult to have confidence in the vitalist project. One response would be to point to various ethnophilosophical accounts of vitality scattered across the literature and argue that those descriptions of vitality in those African cultures do represent the actual ontological ideas within the cultural worldviews after consideration. Any distortions in Tempels' accounts would then fail to rub off on these separate accounts or, at the very least, may not totally undermine them. If true, then the vitalist account reflects an African metaphysical theory, although it would reflect an ontology that needs some critical reconstruction. Friends of the vitalist position might accept this minimal response and move on.

8 The Supernaturalist Critique

For the traditional vitalists, one of the more pressing concerns is responding to criticisms about the nature and/or the reality of the vital force. The critique can be crystallised as follows. If we take it to be true that there exists this ethereal or spiritual energy that emanates from God and is present in all things, then proponents of such a view are admitting a few things: that (1) they possess justifications for holding the view – whether logical or empirical – and that (2) they hold such an understanding of the reality of the vital force that they can state/predict how this energy behaves and what implications may arise from its behaviour. For the vitalist view to work, assumptions (1) and (2) must be shown to be factual. For critics of the vitalist view, both assumptions are, unfortunately, untrue.

In the first instance, critics argue that there are no real justifications for holding the vitalist view except for tradition. Tradition, of course, is not enough – if philosophical discourse is the goal. For instance, there are some who traditionally upheld the view (and for a long time) that the Earth was the centre of the Universe until Copernicus proved the view to be false.

Empirically, the vitalist view fails as we have yet to positively encounter and point to this vital force. Indeed, several attempts to dissect the human body or perform live surgeries on the human body have failed to show that such a thing exists. Furthermore, there has been no indication that such a thing exists in various animals whose anatomy we are aware of. The same applies to plants, rocks, and organisms that exist at the cellular level. Friends of the vitalist view would immediately retort that the vital force is spiritual, so searching for material evidence is fruitless. However, such an argument logically destroys our ability to provide empirical evidence for the phenomenon, so we must depend largely on logical evidence for our justification for the claim. But what is this logical justification? So far, theorists of vitalism have not provided a clear logical justification for the view. Fortunately, one can deduce one such argument/justification from what has been said in the literature. The argument could be as follows: It is true that there is evidence of animation in human beings. While we can point to body parts of all kinds, one cannot point to this factor of animation. Indeed, a fresh human corpse is a good expression of this point, for while the body parts may be intact, the person is dead because that animating character has ceased to exist within the body. Thus, we can plausibly deduce the existence of vitality from the effect it creates – the animation of the human body.[15] Unfortunately, this argument is quite problematic. The main reason for its problematic nature is that the animation of the human body is easily explainable by a simple recourse to neuroscience. We will not explain, in neuroscientific detail, how the central nervous system in human beings works (we do not have the space to do so), but the view is that brain function, along with the neuro-chemical and electrical processes that go on in the central nervous system are the precise reasons why we can will our bodies to move and it does (Churchland, 1981; Dennett, 1991; Churchland, 2002). It is also an injury/injuries to certain parts of this nervous system that ensures that a human corpse or the body of a human person in a vegetative state remains inanimate. If this is true, then the argument from animation fails. If there are good reasons to be severely sceptical of the existence of the vital force, then, empirically or logically[16] speaking, there is little grounding for the view.

The above leads us to the second point (2). If the reality of the vital force is unjustifiable, then it follows that whatever understanding one might have about

---

[15] While this might not be the strongest of arguments, we invite friends of the vitalist view to conceive of a better argument, in order to further the conversation.

[16] Even when one appeals to three-value logical systems like Ezumezu Logic (see Chimakonam, 2019), where seemingly opposed propositions are contextualised or complemented, one must, in the first instance, show that these seemingly opposed propositions are, in themselves, plausible.

the nature, workings, and effects of this vital force is spurious. One cannot, for instance, claim that it is the vital force that grants one dignity or that the pursuit of vitality somehow equates to the pursuit of morality (if it is true that there is no real evidence for the reality of the vital force). What this then means is that original claims made about the nature and functioning of the vital force are neither based on empirical evidence nor logical discernment (per se) but on something else –false propositions.

The failure of these thick (and possibly) false metaphysical propositions has led some to propose a so-called naturalistic version of the vitalist view (see Metz, 2012; Lougheed, 2023), as we have noted earlier in this Element, where things like power and creativity, growth, creative work and increase, and so on, take the place of spiritual energy. However, such a move is not without its problems. These items represent some factual experience, but there are no real reasons to believe that these items should go the extra mile to represent vitality. Occam's razor is not merciful here. For instance, increase, or fertility, simply represents or equates, in one sense, the ability (and expression of the ability) to procreate. Nothing more. What justifications do we have to multiply entities beyond necessity by claiming that fertility implies a show of vitality beyond equating the expression of the ability to procreate? Proponents of the liveliness view have yet to provide an answer to this point.

But there is still one possible move for friends of the vitalist view to make. This involves appeals to physics where energy is considered a sort of non-physical fundamental property of reality, which can neither be created nor destroyed and is transferable from one entity to another in one form (potential, electrical, kinetic, etc.) or the other. It is this energy that drives the human being, even down to the cellular level, and the extreme diminution of this energy could imply death or a different form of being that might be different from the mode of existence that is typical of a healthy and living person. It may very well be the case that this move is viable, and we do not explore it in detail, but the question that remains is whether such a move truly portrays a vision of vitality that equates to the original traditional vision of vitality that the anonymous traditional African philosophers of the Bantu school of thought supposedly had long ago. It is unlikely. However, contemporary African philosophers might find this move plausible and a consideration for future research.

9 Critiquing the Naturalist View

Metz offers a couple of interesting critiques against the vitalist view that proponents of the theory ought to respond to convincingly. His critiques can be summarised or categorised into two main strands – the knowledge critique and the progress critique.

In the first instance, Metz notes that the vitalist theory of meaning fails to account for the sort of meaninglessness (or even anti-meaning) that comes with incorrectly relying on a false belief or the meaningfulness that comes with discovering some novel fact for its own sake. The failure arises from the fact that the augmentation or diminution of vital force does not lie squarely on the possession of knowledge for its own sake or the harbouring of false beliefs. Metz notes:

> A person's life seems less meaningful to some degree, the more he fails to understand, and especially the more he is misguided about, the basics of the world and his place in it. However, such failure to understand need not undercut vitality or community ... part of what is relevant is what the false belief is about, apart from the belief's causal influence on other parts of a life. To see that, consider a case of false belief that does not reduce liveliness, is not likely to reduce it, and might even produce it. If one had radically mistaken views about the origin of the human species, say, one believed that we were put here by the Flying Spaghetti Monster 10 000 years ago, I submit that one's life would be somewhat less meaningful because of that, even if we suppose that no harm came from this belief and that only good feelings sprang from it. (Metz, 2020, pp. 120–121)

In other words, if it were ever the case that some knowledge was false but believed to be true, or that some knowledge had no practical relevance it would seem that the vitalist view would have no explanation as to why possessing such knowledge/beliefs (say believing in the Flying Spaghetti Monster God), in itself, is something that undermines vitality/meaning (when our intuitions tells us that it does). Of course, one could bite the bullet and insist that truth is not relevant for meaning and that the relevant feelings of esteem and admiration (for instance), or the appeal of a religious life as an end that is worth pursuing for its sake, might just be enough. But, as Metz notes, such claims are counterintuitive and may lead one towards a dangerous slippery slope.

Perhaps there is another way out. One assumption that Metz's argument makes is the assumption that only one activity or event (belief in a false God) is the direct and only cause of the effect of an increase in vitality/meaning. But is this really the case? Notice that though the foundational belief is false, and may very well have a negative impact on the life force of the believer, that negative impact may well be overwhelmed by the performance of other activities that are in themselves positive. Suppose that in the community of believers of the flying spaghetti monster, there is a great sense of brotherhood, mutual sharing, love, faith in something, and so on. These activities, on their own, can plausibly increase one's vitality despite whatever decrease might arise from the initial false belief. In this way, it is not that the false belief fails to decrease vitality; it is that other factors/activities increase the individual's vitality beyond the decrease in vitality caused by the false belief. Even the courage to have conviction in one's belief is something that might increase one's vitality, regardless of whether one is holding a false belief or not, and whether that belief decreases or increases one's vitality. It is the same way that certain heroic acts during the Second Gulf War were meaningful, even though it may be true that the war itself was fought on the basis of a lie (that Iraq possessed weapons of mass destruction).

In any case, Metz furthers his critique by pointing out that the vitalist viewpoint cannot properly account for the intuition that there is something more meaningful and/or valuable about, say, Darwin's discovery of evolution than there is about knowing the number of craters on the moon.

In relation to the 'progress' arguments, Metz says the following:

> It is hard to see how either vitality qua liveliness or community qua caring and sharing can explain the importance of novelty relative to what other enquirers have done in the past. One might reply that making such discoveries required enormous amounts of effort and creativity to achieve. One could also point out that having made such discoveries would give those who made them strong feelings of pride and excite many others who learn of the discoveries. These two points direct us to find meaning in the vitalist causes and effects of accomplishments. However, I argue that it is the accomplishments themselves, and not merely their vitalist causes and effects, that also bear real meaning. (Metz, 2020, pp. 121–122)

Notice what is at stake here. For Metz, the vitalist view cannot show why novelty, in itself, is worthy of admiration, or why it is an end worth pursuing for its own sake. The vitalist cause would be something like one's creative power, which allows one to produce the necessary knowledge – but this cause is not the bearer of meaning. If we imagine that a hermit, X, in 2024, discovered, on her own, that the earth revolved around the sun, such an individual would have produced knowledge with her creative power, but it would not be as much of a meaningful contribution to knowledge as Copernicus' contribution of the same kind, which was produced centuries ago.

To respond to this view, one route to go would be to admit that meaning, as per the vitalist view, manifests itself in degrees. But this does not really strike at the heart of Metz's comment, and it only provides a first step. To respond to Metz's point, we appeal to Kirk Lougheed's response to Metz on this issue (Lougheed, 2023). For Lougheed, in order to decipher what makes novelty meaningful in the vitalist view, one can turn to Metz's definition of meaning for clues. Earlier, Metz had defined meaning as follows:

> To ask about meaning, I submit, is to pose questions such as: which ends, beside one's own pleasure as such, are most worth pursuing for their own sake; how to transcend one's animal nature; and what in life merits great esteem or admiration. If a theory is a competent answer to one of these questions, then one should deem it to count as being about meaning in life. (Metz, 2013, p. 34)

For Lougheed, it would be these same variables that would help the vitalist view in deciphering what use of creative power possesses a higher degree of meaning. The argument is that since novel discoveries are inherently worthy of esteem and admiration (since they ultimately lead to unprecedented progress), worth pursuing for their own sake (since knowledge is presumably worth pursuing for its own sake) and inherently transcend our animal nature (in this context, our base use of our cognitive abilities), any product of novelty that is borne from the Godlike property of consciousness, rationality and/or creativity is inherently more meaningful than non- novel knowledge. If a person were able to count and know the number of blades of grass in her backyard, such knowledge would be presumably less meaningful than knowledge about what precisely cures cancer. The novelty of the latter discovery naturally elicits more esteem and admiration (for instance) than the former discovery. Thus, even if one could argue that both pursuits elicit some sort of self-realisation, it could also be true that the sort of self-realisation that comes with the latter example is stronger, for the reasons outlined above.

Concluding his critique, Metz (2020) observes that the vitalist view fails to show how a repetitive life is less meaningful than one that is not a repetitive one – especially when one is unaware of that repetitiveness. This is, admittedly, a difficult point to respond to, but we will say that the problem is by no means peculiar to the vitalist view (and, in fact, generally haunts accounts of life's meaning). One way that friends of the vitalist view might respond, however, is by claiming that life, even if repetitive, remains meaningful, insofar as that repetitiveness fails to undermine the individual's vitality in some other way. For instance, if one were to pursue a moment of meaning repetitively in such a way that the discovery of that repetition drains that individual's creative power or depresses the individual, then that sort of repetitive pursuit eventually undermines vitality (especially if the loss of vitality from depression or the draining of one's creative power overwhelms whatever gains are achieved by repetitive pursuits). This would also mean that repetitive pursuits that fail to cause a strain, even due to ignorance, would not be meaningless after all, and the vitalist might bite the bullet in this way. Of course, proponents of the vitalist view may, in the future, provide a more robust response to Metz's view, and these arguments are worth examining.

Conclusion

What we have done so far, in this Element, is to provide the reader with not just an overview of the notion of vitality but a critical analysis of one of the more important concepts in African theology and philosophy of religion. We began by examining and reconstructing, in Part I, three important traditional views of the notion of vitality, viz. the Bantu, Yoruba, and Igbo conceptions of vitality, as championed by various scholars in those traditions. Here, Tempels' examination of Bantu vitalist ontology was discussed, and the concepts of *ase* and *ndu* were introduced as concepts that delineated vitality in the Yoruba and Igbo views, respectively. Next, we discussed vitalist ethics, where we crystallised the vitalist theory of right action into the following terse statement: 'An action is morally acceptable insofar as it augments one's vitality, and an action is morally wrong insofar as it diminishes one's vitality (or the vitality of others), except in cases where self-defence is necessary.' We also explored the vitalist theory of dignity and meaning, based on traditional notions of vitality and the liveliness view. Finally, we examined some important critiques of vitality from scholars like Innocent Asouzu, Bernard Matolino, Thaddeus Metz, and so on. Here, questions about the racial foundations of the view, the spirituality that strongly undergirds the view, and its seeming inability to ground the value of progress and knowledge for its sake were examined, and tentative responses were provided.

This Element is far from exhaustive, given the required length for this Element, and we anticipate that many important discussions have not been addressed by the Element but part of the purpose of this project is to introduce specialists and non-specialists in African philosophy to an important concept in traditional African metaphysics, and also inspire more critical engagements with various aspects of the view. Thus, this Element serves as an initial stepping stone for more research in this area of African philosophy.

References

Abimbola, K. (2006). *Yoruba Culture: A Philosophical Account*. Great Britain: Iroko Academic Publishers.

Abimbola, W. (1971). 'The Yoruba Concept of Human Personality' in *La Notion de Personne en Afrique Noire*. Collogues Intemationaux de Centre National de la Recherche Scientifique. Paris: Centre National de la Recherche Scientifique. No. 544: 73–89.

Abiodun, R. (1994). Understanding Yoruba Art and Aesthetics: The Concept of Ase. *African Arts*, 27 (3): 68–102.

Agada, A. (2019). Rethinking the Metaphysical Questions of the Mind, Matter, Freedom, Determinism, Purpose and the Mind-Body Problem within the Panpsychist Framework of Consolation. *South African Journal of Philosophy*, 38 (1), pp. 1–16.

Agada, A. (2020a). The African vital force theory of meaning in life. *South African Journal of Philosophy*, 39(2): 100–112.

Agada, A. (2020b). Grounding the Consolationist Concept of Mood in the African Vital Force Theory. *Philosophia Africana*, 19(2): 101–121.

Agada, A. (2022). *Consolationism and Comparative African Philosophy: Beyond Universalism and Particularism*. New York: Routledge.

Aleke, P. A. (2022). Being and Force: An Exploration in Classical and African Metaphysics. *Phronimon*, 22(8957): 1–19.

Anyanwu, K. C. (1984). The Meaning of Ultimate Reality in Igbo Cultural Experience. *Ultimate Reality and Meaning (URAM)*, 7(2): 84–101.

Arazu, R. (1978). *A Cultural Model for Christian Prayer, African Christian Spirituality*. London: Chapman.

Asouzu, I. (2004). *Methods and Principles of Complementary Reflection in and Beyond African Philosophy*. Calabar: University of Calabar Press.

Asouzu, I. (2011). Ibuanyidanda (Complementary Reflection), Communalism and Theory Formulation in African Philosophy. *Thought and Practice: A Journal of the Philosophical Association of Kenya (PAK), New Series*, 3(2): 9–34.

Asouzu, I. A. (2007a). *Ibuanyidanda: New Complementary Ontology, beyond World- Immanentism, Ethnocentric Reduction and Imposition*. London: Transaction.

Asouzu, I. A. (2007b). *Ibuaru:* The Heavy Burden of Philosophy beyond African Philosophy. London: Transaction.

Attoe, A. (2020). A Systematic Account of African Conceptions of the Meaning of/in Life. *South African Journal of Philosophy*, 39(2): 127–139.

References

Attoe, A. (2022). *Groundwork for a New Kind of African Metaphysics: The Idea of Singular Complementarity*. Cham: Palgrave Macmillan.

Attoe, A. (2023). *The Question of Life's Meaning: An African Perspective*. Cham: Palgrave Macmillan.

Awolalu, J. O & Dopamu, P. A (2005). *West African Traditional Religion*. Nigeria: Macmillan Nigeria.

Balogun, O. A. (2007). The Concepts of Ori and Human Destiny in Traditional Yoruba Thought: A Soft-Deterministic Interpretation. *Nordic Journal of African Studies*, 16(1): 116–130

Barber, K. (1981). How Man Makes God in West Africa: Yoruba Attitudes Towards the 'Orisa'. *Africa: Journal of the International African Institute*, 51(3): 724–745.

Bascom, W. (1991). *Ifa Divination: Communication between Gods and Men in West Africa*. Bloomington: Indiana University Press.

Bergson, H. (2023). *Creative Evolution*. Translated by Donald A. Landes. London: Routledge.

Bikopo, D. & van Bogaert, L.-J. (2010). Reflection on Euthanasia: Western and African Ntomba Perspectives on the Death of a King. *Developing World Bioethics*, 10(1): 42–48.

Bolduc, G. (2023). On the Heuristic Value of Hans Driesch's Vitalism. In Donohue, C. & Wolfe, C. T. (eds.), *Vitalism and Its Legacy in Twentieth Century Life Sciences and Philosophy*. pp. 27–48. Cham: Springer.

Chang, K. (2011). Alchemy as Studies of Life and Matter: Reconsidering the Place of Vitalism in Early Modern Chymistry. *Isis*, 102(2): 322–329.

Chimakonam, J. (2014). *History of African Philosophy*. Retrieved June 9, 2018, from Internet Encyclopedia of Philosophy: www.iep.utm.edu/afric-hi/.

Chimakonam, J. (2019). *Ezumezu: A System of Logic for African Philosophy and Studies*. Cham: Switzerland.

Chimakonam, J. O. & Lucky Uchenna Ogbonnaya, L. U. (2015). A Conceptual and Contextual Meaning of 'Mmadu' in the Igbo Reality Scheme: Further Contribution to URAM Igbo Studies. *Ultimate Reality and Meaning (URAM)*, 34(3–4): 268–285.

Churchland, P. (1981). Eliminative Materialism and the Propositional Attitudes. *Journal of Philosophy*, 68(2): 67–90.

Churchland, P. (2002). *Brain-Wise*. Massachusetts: The MIT Press.

Cimino, G. & Duchesneau, F. (eds.) (1997), *Vitalisms: From Haller to the Cell Theory:Proceedings of the Zaragoza Symposium*. Florence: L.S. Olschki.

Dennett, D. (1991). *Consciousness Explained*. New York: Back Bay Books.

Driesch, H. (1914). *The History and Theory of Vitalism*. London: Macmillan.

References

Drewal, H.J., Pemberton III, J., & Abiodun, R. (1989). *Yoruba. Nine Centuries of African Art and Thought*. New York: The Center for African Art, in association with Harry N. Abrams Publishers.

Drewal, H. J. (Online). Às̩e̩ and the Senses in Understandings of Yorùbá Arts and Culture. In Clarke, C. (ed.), *Arts of Global Africa*. New Jersey: The Newark Museum Collection. https://newarkmuseumart.org/wp-content/uploads/2023/04/NMOA-As-%CC%87e-%CC%87-Drewal-essay_v2.pdf.

Drewal, M. T. (1992). *Yoruba Ritual: Performers, Play, Agency*. Bloomington: Indiana University Press. https://books.google.co.za/books?id=vxXvi8WhrrMC&pg=PA1&source=gbs_toc_r&cad=2#v=onepage&q&f=false.

Dzobo, N. (1992). Values in a Changing Society: Man, Ancestors and God. In Wiredu, K. & Gyekye, K. (eds.), *Person and Community: Ghanian Philosophical Studies*. pp. 223–240. Washington: Center for Research in Values and Philosophy.

Edeh, E. (1985). *Towards an Igbo Metaphysics*. Chicago: Loyola University Press.

Fayemi, A.K. (2007). The Concept of 'Olodumare' in Yoruba Language: An Exercise in Conceptual Decolonisation. In Ike Odimegwu et al. (eds.), *Philosophy, Democracy and Conflicts in Africa*. Akwa: Department of Philosophy, pp. 301–314.

Garrett, B. (2013). Vitalism Versus Emergent Materialism. In Normandin, S. & Wolfe, C. T. (eds.), *Vitalism and the Scientific Image in Post-Enlightenment Life Science*, 1800–2010. pp. 127–154. Cham: Springer.

Gbadegesin, S. (2004). Towards a Theory of Destiny. In Wiredu, K. (ed.), *Companion to African Philosophy*. pp. 314–323. Oxford: Blackwell.

Haigh, E. (1985). Vital Forces and Vital Laws in Eighteenth-Century French Physiology. *Man and Nature/L'homme et la nature*, 4: 1–15. https://doi.org/10.7202/1011833ar.

Haigh, E. L. (1977). The Vital Principle of Paul Joseph Barthez: The Clash between Monism and Dualism. *Medical History*, 21: 1–14.

Hallen, B. & Sodipo, J. O. (1986). *Knowledge, Belief and Witchcraft*. London: Ethnographical.

Hallgren, R. (1995). *The Vital Force. A Study of Àse in the Traditional and Neo-Traditional Culture of the Yoruba People*. Lund: Lund Studies in African and Asian Religions.

Harvey, M. L. (2015). Deity from a Python, Earth from a Hen, Humankind from Mystery: Narrative and Knowledge in Yorùbá Cosmology. *Estudos de Religião*, 29(2): 237–270.

Hountondji, P. J. (1983). *African Philosophy: Myth and Reality*. Bloomington: Indiana University Press.

Hountondji, P. (1996). *African philosophy: Myth and Reality*. Indiana: Indiana University Press.

Ibeabuchi, O. M. (2013). The Theory of Forces as Conceived by Igbo-Africans. *Filosofia Theoretica: Journal of African Philosophy, Culture and Religion*, 2(1): 289–313.

Idowu, E. B. (1962). *Olodumare: God in Yoruba Belief*. London: Longmans.

Idowu, E. B. (1973). *African Traditional Religion: A Definition*. London: SCM Press Ltd.

Imafidon, E., Matolino, B. O. L., Agada, A., Attoe, A., & Mangena, F. (2019). Are We Finished with the Ethnophilosophy Debate? A Multi-Perspective Conversation. *Filosofia Theoretica: Journal of African Philosophy, Culture and Religions*, 8(2): 111–137.

Isiguzo, A. I., Ukagba, G., & Otakpor, N. (2004). The Igbo Concept of a Person. *Africa: Rivista trimestrale di studi e documentazione dell'Istituto italiano per l'Africae l'Oriente*, 59(2): 231–243.

Isola, J. A. (1998). Olodumare: God in Yoruba Belief and the Theistic Problem of Evil. *African Studies Quarterly*, 2(1): 1–17.

Kagame, A. (1956). *La Philosophie Bantu-Rwandaise de I'etre*. Brussels: Académie Royale des Sciences Coloniales.

Kagame, A. (1989). The Problem of 'Man' in Bantu Philosophy. *Journal of African Religion and Philosophy*, 1(1): 35–40.

Kasenene, P. (1994). Ethics in African Theology. In Villa-Vicencio, C. & de Gruchy, J. (eds.), *Doing Ethics in Context: South African Perspectives*. pp. 138–147. Cape Town: David Philip.

Laval, B. (2005). Divinity, Creativity and Humanity in Yoruba Aesthetics. *Literature & Aesthetics*, 15(1): 161–174.

Lajul, W. (2017). African Metaphysics: Traditional and Modern Discussions. In I. Ukpokolo (Ed.), *Themes, Issues and Problems in African Philosophy*. Cham: Palgrave Macmillian, pp. 19–48.

Levy-Bruhl (1926). *How Natives Think*. London: Allen and Unwin.

Lougheed, K. (2023). Liveliness as a Theory of Meaning in Life: Problems and Prospects. *Journal of the American Philosophical Association*, 10 (4): pp. 797–813.

Lougheed, K., Molefe, M., & Metz, T. (2024). *African Philosophy of Religion and Western Monotheism*. Cambridge: Cambridge University Press.

Magesa, L. (1997). *African Religion: The Moral Traditions of Abundant Life*. New York: Orbis Books.

Makinde, M. A. (1984). An African Concept of Human Personality: The Yoruba Example. *Ultimate Reality and Meaning*, 7(3): 189–200.

References

Matolino, B. (2011). Tempels' Philosophical Racialism. *South African Journal of Philosophy*, 30(3): 330–342. https://doi.org/10.4314/sajpem.v30i3.69579.

McKenzie, P. R. (1976). Yoruba Òrìṣà Cults: Some Marginal Notes concerning Their Cosmology and Concepts of Deity. *Journal of Religion in Africa*, 8(3): 189–207.

Mclaughlin, B. (2003). Vitalism and Emergence. In Baldwin, T. (ed.), *The Cambridge History of Philosophy 1870–1945*. pp. 631–639. Cambridge: Cambridge University Press.

Metz, T. (2012). African Conceptions of Human Dignity: Vitality and Community as the Ground of Human Rights. *Human Rights Review*, 13(1): 19–37.

Metz, T. (2012). An African Theory of Moral Status: A Relational Alternative to Individualism and Holism. *Ethical Theory and Moral Practice*, 15: 387–402.

Metz, T. (2013). *Meaning in Life*. Oxford: Oxford University press.

Metz, T. (2020). African Theories of Meaning in Life: A Critical Assessment. *South African Journal of Philosophy*, 39(2): 113–126.

Metz, T. (2022). *A Relational Moral Theory: African Ethics in and Beyond the Continent*. Oxford: Oxford University Press.

Mkhize, N. (2008). Ubuntu and Harmony: An African Approach to Morality and Ethics. In Nicolson, R. (ed.), *Persons in Community: African Ethics in a Global Culture*. pp. 35–44. Pietermaritzburg: University of KwaZulu-Natal Press.

Mlungwana, Y. (2020). An African Approach to the Meaning of Life. *South African Journal of Philosophy*, 39(2): 153–165.

Molefe, M. (2017). An African Religious Ethics and the Euthyphro Problem. *Acta Academica: Critical Views on Society, Culture and Politics*, 49(1): 22–38.

Molefe, M. (2018). African Metaphysics and Religious Ethics. *Filosofia Theoretica: Journal of African Philosophy, Culture and Religions*, 7(3): 19–37.

Molefe, M. (2020). *An African Ethics of Personhood and Bioethics: A Reflection on Abortion and Euthanasia*. Cham: Palgrave Macmillan.

Molefe, M. (2022). *Human Dignity in African Philosophy: A Very Short Introduction*. Cham: Springer.

Morakinyo, O. & Akiwowo A. (1981). The Yoruba ontology of personality and motivation: A multidisciplinary approach. *Journal of Social and Biological Structures*, 4(1): 19–38.

Mullen, N. (2004). *Yoruba Art and Culture*. In Winn, L. M. and Jacknis, I. (eds.), Hearst Museum of Anthropology and the Regents of the University Of California. Berkeley: Phoebe A.

Nalwamba, K. & Buitendag, J. (2017). Vital Force as a Triangulated Concept of Nature and s(S)pirit. *HTS Teologiese Studies/Theological Studies*, 73(3): 1–10.

Negedu, I.A. (2014). Beyond the Four Categories of African Philosophy. *International Journal of African Society Cultures and Traditions*, 2(3): 10–19.

Ngangah, I. C. (2019). Vital Force, Personhood, and Community in African Philosophy: An Ontological Study. *The International Journal of Humanities & Social Studies*, 7(10): 48–55. DOI:10.24940/theijhss/2019/v7/i10/HS1910-023.

Njoku, F. O. (2002). *Essays in African Philosophy, Thought and Theology*. Owerri: Snaap Press.

Ofuasia, E. (2024). *Iwa: The Process-Relational Dimension to African Metaphysics*. Cham: Springer.

Ofuasia, E. & Ibiyemi, S. O. (2024). An Inquiry into the 'Maleness' of God in African Traditional Religions: The Igbo and Yorùbá as Illustrations. *Journal of Africana Religions*, 12(1): 86–103. https://doi.org/10.5325/jafrireli.12.1.0086.

Ofuasia, E. (2020). Monotheism and metaphysics in the *yorùbá* thought system: A Process Alternative. *JOCAP*, 1: 43–58.

Ogbonnaya, L. (2014). The Question of 'Being' in African Philosophy. *Filosofia Theoretica: Journal of African Philosophy, Culture and Religions*, 3(1): 108–126.

Okafor, E. N. (2020). The Concept of Chi in the Igbo Philosophy of the Person. *Prajñā Vihāra*, 21(2): 62–81.

Okafor, S. O. (1982). Bantu Philosophy: Placide Tempels Revisited. *Journal of Religion in Africa*, 13(2): 83–100.

Okoro, C. I. & Emedolu, C. C. (2020). Relations between Self and Vital Force in Igbo Context. *Sapientia Foundation Journal of Education, Sciences and Gender Studies (SFJESGS)*, 2(2): 128–136.

Onunwa, U. (2012). A Handbook of African Religion and Cultures. Lagos: Udi Global Resources.

Oyeshile, O. (2021). Yoruba Philosophy of Existence, *Iwa* (Character) and Contemporary Socio-Political Order. *Philosophia: International Journal of Philosophy*, 22(1): 1–18.

Pele, A. (2016). Kant on Human Dignity: A Critical Approach. *Espaço Jurídico Journal of Law*, 17(2): 493–512.

Posteraro, T. S. (2023). Vitalism and the Problem of Individuation: Another Look at Bergson's *Élan Vital*. In Donohue, C. and Wolfe, C. T. (eds.), *Vitalism and Its Legacy in Twentieth-Century Life Sciences and Philosophy*. pp. 9–26. Cham: Springer.

Ramose, M. B. (1999). *African Philosophy through Ubuntu*. Harare: Mond Books.

Roothaan, A. & Bello, S. A. (2024). Genealogies of Vital Force: 'Ntu', 'Àṣẹ', and Conceptual Lines of Descent. *Journal of Comparative Literature and Aesthetics*, 47(1): 63–74.

References

Spaulding, E. G. (1906). Driesch's Theory of Vitalism. *The Philosophical Review*, 15(5): 518–527.

Stollberg, G. (2000). Vitalism and Vital Force in Life Sciences – The Demise and Life of a Scientific Conception. *Bielefeld Institute for Global Society Studies*. https://citeseerx.ist.psu.edu/document?repid=rep1&type=pdf&doi=03699aed1f6ead09c2287faa1016e5369a40394d.

Taye, O. R. (2013). Questionable but Unquestioned Beliefs: A Call for a Critical Examination of Yoruba Culture. *Thought and Practice: A Journal of the Philosophical Association of Kenya (PAK)*, New Series, 5(2): 81–101.

Tempels, P. (1959). *Bantu Philosophy*. Trans. King C. Paris: Presence Africaine.

Thornhill, J. T. (2020). A Vitalism Ethos and the Chiropractic Health Care Paradigm. *Journal of Chiropractic Humanities*, 27(C): 59–81.

Uzukwu, B. (1982). Igbo World and Ultimate Reality and Meaning. *Ultimate Reality and Meaning (URAM)*, 5(3): 188–209.

Vega, M. M. (1999). The Ancestral Sacred Creative Impulse of Africa and the African Diaspora: Ase, the Nexus of the Black Global Aesthetic. *Lenox Avenue: A Journal of Interarts Inquiry*, 5: 45–57.

Weidtmann, N. (2019). The Philosophy of Ubuntu and the Notion of Vital Force. In Ogude, J. (ed.), *Ubuntu and the Reconstitution of Community*. pp. 98–113. Bloomington: Indiana University Press.

Wolfe, C. (2022). Vitalism. In Kirchhoff, T. (ed.), *Online Encyclopedia Philosophy of Nature*, pp. 1–9. https://doi.org/10.11588/oepn.2022.2.87350.

Acknowledgement

This work was supported by the Faculty Research and Innovation Committee, University of the Witwatersrand (grant number AATTO24). Many thanks to the peer reviewer of this work for their insightful comments.

Cambridge Elements⁼

Global Philosophy of Religion

Yujin Nagasawa
University of Oklahoma

Yujin Nagasawa is Kingfisher College Chair of the Philosophy of Religion and Ethics and Professor of Philosophy at the University of Oklahoma. He is the author of *The Problem of Evil for Atheists* (2024), *Maximal God: A New Defence of Perfect Being Theism* (2018), *Miracles: A Very Short Introduction* (2018), *The Existence of God: A Philosophical Introduction* (2011), and *God and Phenomenal Consciousness* (2008), along with numerous articles. He is the editor-in-chief of *Religious Studies* and served as the president of the British Society for the Philosophy of Religion from 2017 to 2019.

About the Series

This Cambridge Elements series provides concise and structured overviews of a wide range of religious beliefs and practices, with an emphasis on global, multi-faith viewpoints. Leading scholars from diverse cultural backgrounds and geographical regions explore topics and issues that have been overlooked by Western philosophy of religion.

Cambridge Elements

Global Philosophy of Religion

Elements in the Series

Afro-Brazilian Religions
José Eduardo Porcher

The African Mood Perspective on God and the Problem of Evil
Ada Agada

Contemporary Pagan Philosophy
Eric Steinhart

Semi-Secular Worldviews and the Belief in Something Beyond
Carl-Johan Palmqvist and Francis Jonbäck

Zoroastrianism and Contemporary Philosophy
Daniel Nolan

Karma and Rebirth in Hinduism
Swami Medhananda

Religious Naturalism
John Bishop and Ken Perszyk

The Notion of Vitality in African Philosophy of Religion
Aribiah David Attoe and Amara Esther Chimakonam

A full series listing is available at: www.cambridge.org/EGPR

For EU product safety concerns, contact us at Calle de José Abascal, 56–1º,
28003 Madrid, Spain or eugpsr@cambridge.org.

www.ingramcontent.com/pod-product-compliance
Lightning Source LLC
LaVergne TN
LVHW020006080526
838200LV00081B/4402